Borders, Bras and Battles

A Practical Guide to Mentor Undergraduate
Women to Achieve Career Success

La Vonne I. Neal, Ph.D.
Sarah Militz-Frielink, M.S.Ed.
Alicia L. Moore, Ph.D.
Karina Avila
Maria Colompos
Shanell Walter

Borders, Bras and Battles

A Practical Guide to Mentor Undergraduate
Women to Achieve Career Success

La Vonne I. Neal, Ph.D.
Sarah Militz-Frielink, M.S.Ed.
Alicia L. Moore, Ph.D.
Karina Avila
Maria Colompos
Shanell Walter

Apprentice House
Loyola University Maryland
Baltimore, Maryland

First Edition

Printed in the United States of America

Paperback ISBN: 978-1-62720-110-0
E-book ISBN: 978-1-62720-111-7

Design: Apprentice House
Published by Apprentice House

Apprentice House
Loyola University Maryland
4501 N. Charles Street
Baltimore, MD 21210
410.617.5265 • 410.617.2198 (fax)
www.ApprenticeHouse.com
info@ApprenticeHouse.com

ACKNOWLEDGEMENTS

We thank all of the faculty, staff, and scholars at Northern Illinois University (NIU) for their unwavering support during the completion of this project—especially the College of Education, the Department of Military Science, and President Douglas Baker and his Leadership Team. We are grateful to the NIU ROTC Huskie Battalion for making this research a possibility. A special thanks to the University of Illinois at Chicago and Southwestern University for providing cross-university collaboration on this project.

We also give a special thanks to the United States Air Force Academy, the United States Army Command and General Staff College, the National Association for Multicultural Education (NAME), the Association of Black Women in Higher Education (ABWHE), and the Association for the Study of African American Life and History (ASALH) for providing forums for us to share our research findings.

A special thanks to all of our family members and loved ones who supported us during the long hours of research, writing, and travel to present at conferences.

Spanish

Agradecemos a todos los profesores, el personal y los académicos en la Universidad Northern Illinois (NIU), por su apoyo incondicional durante la realización de este proyecto, especialmente la Facultad de Educación, el Departamento de Ciencias Militares, y el presidente Douglas Baker y su equipo de liderazgo. Estamos muy agradecidos a la NIU ROTC Huskie Batallón para hacer esta investigación una posibilidad. Un agradecimiento especial a la Universidad de Illinois en Chicago y la Universidad Southwestern para proporcionar la colaboración entre la universidad en este proyecto.

También damos un agradecimiento especial a la academia de fuerza aérea de Estados Unidos, el Comando de Estados Unidos Ejército y Estado Mayor, la Asociación Nacional para la Educación Multicultural (NAME), la Asociación de Mujeres Negras de la Educación Superior (ABWHE), y la Asociación para el Estudio de la Vida e Historia del Áfricano Americano (ASALH) para proporcionar foros para nosotros para compartir nuestros hallazgos de la investigación.

Un agradecimiento especial a todos nuestros familiares y seres queridos que nos apoyaron durante las largas horas de investigación, la escritura y los viajes para presentar en conferencias.

Greek

Ευχαριστούμε όλους του σχολή, το προσωπικό, και τους μελετητές στο Northern Illinois University (NIU) για την αμέριστη υποστήριξή τους κατά τη διάρκεια της ολοκλήρωσης του έργου αυτού, ειδικά το Κολέγιο της Εκπαίδευσης, του Τμήματος Στρατιωτικής Επιστήμης και Πρόεδρος Ντάγκλας Baker και Ηγετικής Ομάδας του. Είμαστε ευγνώμονες στην NIU ROTC Huskie Τάγμα για την πραγματοποίηση αυτής της έρευνας η δυνατότητα. Ένα ιδιαίτερο ευχαριστώ στο Πανεπιστήμιο του Ιλινόις στο Σικάγο και του Πανεπιστημίου Νοτιοδυτική για την παροχή cross-πανεπιστημιακή συνεργασία σε αυτό το έργο.

Δίνουμε επίσης ιδιαίτερες ευχαριστίες προς τις Ηνωμένες Πολιτείες Σχολή Ικάρων, τις Ηνωμένες Πολιτείες Στρατού Διοίκησης και Γενικού Επιτελείου κολλέγιο, την Εθνική Ένωση για τη Διαπολιτισμική Εκπαίδευση (NAME), του Συλλόγου των μαύρων γυναικών στην Τριτοβάθμια Εκπαίδευση (ABWHE), και του Συνδέσμου για μελέτη της αφρικανικής αμερικανικής ζωής και της ιστορίας (ASALH) για την παροχή φόρουμ για να μοιραστούμε τα ευρήματα της έρευνας μας.

Ένα ιδιαίτερο ευχαριστώ σε όλα τα μέλη της οικογένειας μας και τους αγαπημένους που μας υποστήριξαν κατά τη διάρκεια των πολλών ωρών της έρευνας, τη γραφή, τα ταξίδια και να παρουσιάσει σε συνέδρια.

CONTENTS

FOREWORD
Border Crossers: Fostering Community with Care and Courage

By Conra D. Gist

How do you stand upright in a crooked room? Melissa Harris-Perry describes a type of crooked room phenomenon based on field dependence studies where people adjust their physical positioning based on their perceptions of the surrounding environment.[1] She argues that Black women can often experience society as a crooked room of stereotypes and manipulations telling them to align with harmful images and practices around them.[2] Despite perceiving and experiencing this context, women from marginalized communities must find pathways and tools to see themselves as possessing unrestricted potentialities that neutralize the potency of these crippling paradigms. This often requires women to integrate an array of emancipatory weapons such as critical theoretical perspectives, participating in justice-oriented organizations, and engaging in diverse communities of practice that uplift and fortify them as actualized human beings.

For those committed to working towards justice in educational and military institutions, *Borders, Bras, and Battles* models how to guide a diverse group of women to stand up in a crooked room through critical consciousness grounded in action-oriented leadership and authentic community. As a hopeful vision of what the fight for equality can look like in institutions, *Borders, Bras, and Battles* represents a fusion of personal testimonies, critical and philosophical stances for mentorship, and practical interventions for empowering and nurturing character and leadership capacity. Both the military and higher education institutions are marked by policies, practices, and ideologies that limit access and full participation for some groups. These marks are most clearly visible when power and privilege is used to reproduce inequality and create new operations of oppression. Although these institutional operations can, in part, function in ways that erect borders between people, we—scholars, teachers, leaders, activists, executives, community organizers, visionaries, warriors, dreamers, believers, innovators, builders—can develop creative and impactful ways to act as border crossers.

In 2014, the National Association for Multicultural Education (NAME) called on multiculturalists to generate the capacity for social change by fostering community with care and courage. The scholars' stories offered in this book, along with the practical strategies for mentoring and institutional support, exhibit what is possible when leaders in positions of power make the choice to pierce through a web of institutional inequality facing women who are diverse. As well, the scholars' stories shed light on leaders who are courageous and caring enough to create a network that is poised to nurture the scholars as agents of change as they resist oppressive systems through communities of resistance. When describing the transformative power of organic "communities of resistance", bell hooks asserts the following about those communities:

> [they] emerge around our own struggles for personal self-recovery as well as our efforts to organize collectively to bring about social change...no level of individual self-actualization alone can sustain the marginalized and oppressed. We must be linked to collective struggle, to communities of resistance that

move us outward, into the world.[3]

By answering the call to "link to collective struggle" through mentorship in the context of a community of resistance, the stories of the women in this book reflect newfound courage and agency that allows them to envision productive and transgressive possibilities for their lives. The cross-institutional and interdisciplinary backgrounds characterizing this work are emblematic of the type of border crossing that is possible when action-oriented leadership emerges.

The battleground of equality in institutions involves a matrix of tactics that include challenging specific systems. Similarly, *Borders, Bras, and Battles* offers potential pathways to battlegrounds for justice equality through an endarkened feminist mentor program that engages women in a scholar community of practice via participatory action research that incorporates tools supporting academic and professional advancement. Some of these practices include research courses, conference presentations, writing articles, book chapters, and books, assuming leadership roles, and being prepared to navigate barriers to their holistic success (e.g., economic, professional, health, familial) in the future. The efforts of these bold leaders do not represent the beginning and end of pathways for justice in military and higher education institutions, but rather, should draw you closer to envisioning, embracing and moving towards what is possible in the hope and work of creating more just institutions for future generations. These are the leaders who take seriously the call to become new script writers—the ones who are unafraid of challenging the status quo; the ones who are ridding society of harmful images and practices that surround marginalized groups; the ones who have become the new cultural producers of this age. Yet they face extraordinary bureaucratic pressures within today's educational system, which has increasingly adopted a neoliberal approach toward selectively quantifying experiences.

Maxine Greene suggests that this preference towards selective data sets used to explain the state of affairs in education, can, at times, confine imaginative possibilities. She explains:

> ...the view from a bureaucratic or any other distance makes us see in terms of trends, tendencies, and theoretically predictable events. Whenever we are shown a report or a statistical account of what is happening within a school district or the system as a whole, this becomes evident. It is as if automatic processes were at work; it seems impossible to look at things as if they could be otherwise. When, however, a person chooses to view herself or himself in the midst of things, as beginner or learner or explorer, and has the imagination to envisage new things emerging, more and more begins to seem possible.[4]

As an inspirational and practical guide, the pages that follow in *Borders, Bras, and Battles* give courage to those ready to build new mentor programs that break barriers and cultivate justice practices in military and higher education institutions. May those who read this book find the courage to work towards dismantling the crooked rooms in their institutions, and advance the bold yet unrealized vision of a free and open democratic society.

CHAPTER 1
Answering the Call for Mentorship: U.S. Army ROTC Cadets' Reflections

Our "Endarkened Feminist Mentor Program," is a caring community including three mentors from three different universities and three U.S. Army ROTC female cadets / scholars who are culturally, linguistically, and/or ethnically diverse (CLED). To optimize our scholars' career success, we traverse institutional borders and infuse interdisciplinary backgrounds because we value the collective power of three plus three to win social justice battles to unrestrict potential.

Mentors	Mentees
La Vonne I. Neal, Ph.D.	Cadet Karina Avila
Sarah Militz-Frielink, M.S.Ed.	Cadet Maria Colompos
Alicia L. Moore, Ph.D.	Cadet Shanell Walter

Mentors:

Dr. La Vonne I. Neal Associate Vice President, Northern Illinois University (NIU) & Formerly, Dean of the College of Education, NIU / U.S. Army veteran—Military Intelligence officer/U.S. Army ROTC Alumna.

Primary role as mentor: Provide strategic career success guidance to scholars as they navigate both academic and military missions. Design and facilitate mentoring sessions with scholars.

Sarah Militz-Frielink, M.S.Ed. Doctoral candidate at the University of Illinois at Chicago (UIC) /Adjunct Faculty and Research Assistant at NIU.

Primary role as mentor: Provide research and writing support to scholars. Implement day-to-day operations under Dr. Neal's direction (e.g., teach research courses, structure writing assignments, editing, and conference presentation preparation).

Dr. Alicia L. Moore Cargill Endowed Professor of Education at Southwestern University, Georgetown, TX / Member of the U.S. Army Command and General Staff College Advisory Board.

Primary role as mentor: Provide ongoing academic support to include graduate school admissions and career readiness as defined by the U.S. Army Command and General Staff College.

Mentees:

Karina Avila
Army ROTC cadet / scholar at NIU

Maria Colompos
Army ROTC cadet / scholar at NIU

Shanell Walter
Army ROTC cadet / scholar at NIU

While reviewing research on mentoring best practices, research has shown that having a mentor is one of the most important experiences for women who are CLED who want to pursue careers in academia.[5] Several studies on mentoring in the U.S. military have also espoused the benefits of having a mentoring relationship.[6] The majority of studies and cross-disciplinary reviews of mentoring research have consistently revealed that mentoring has had significant positive correlations with work performance, personal health, quantity of interpersonal relationships, greater career recognition, and general career competence.[7] Despite these benefits, however, the majority of mentoring studies also point to the need for more work to be done in the areas of mentoring definitions, frameworks, and programming.[8] [9] [10]

Our book addresses these gaps in the literature by providing an innovative mentoring program using an empowering theoretical framework—endarkened feminist epistemology.[11] Throughout this book we share insights and wisdom from female military leaders of color (veterans) whom we interviewed while conducting a research study titled: "Borders, Bras, and Battles: Sociocultural Perspectives of Female Scholars of Color in ROTC." It is through their personal testimonies, philosophical stances on mentorship and leadership interventions that readers will develop a greater awareness of the ways in which they can become agents of change in their community with care and courage. To define sociocultural, we drew upon Lev Vygotsky's sociocultural theory, which is "based on the concept that human activities take place in cultural contexts, are mediated by language and other symbol systems, and can best be understood when investigated in their historical development."[12] This book also integrates the perspectives of our ROTC undergraduates—including the high impact practices, which help spark their genius, facilitate engaged learning, support their successful research, publications and the establishment of their professional brand.

We infused personal narratives throughout this manuscript from the aforementioned research study. Their stories are representative of women who are at the beginning of their military and academic careers and women who are successful university and military leaders (e.g., military veterans who are also university faculty or administrators). Together their stories reveal the courage it takes to go beyond the self—to go past one's physical, emotional, and spiritual limits. One may argue that all great, female leaders in the military have embodied this rare care and courage —especially the participants in our study, who became the first to attain positions historically occupied by men (e.g. an African American & member of the 1st cohort of women admitted to the U.S. Air Force Academy; and one of our book co-authors—the first female cadet and first Hispanic female to command an Army ROTC battalion at Northern Illinois University). It takes more than courage to go to the end of one's self; to push past one's breaking point, and as the chapters of this book unfold, you will learn what that is, and how mentoring plays a role in all of this.

For women in the military, for teachers, leaders, activists, executives, community organizers, visionaries, innovators, and for people who often face overwhelming barriers when effecting social change at the institutional and community level—this book is more than a testament to a mentoring program that changed the lives of three female ROTC scholars who are CLED, it is a practical life guide filled with wisdom. This is also an inspiring story about border crossers who overcame many of the same obstacles when crossing socially constructed borders of power and privilege.[13] As the pages of the story will reveal, we included a synthesis of the literature on undergraduate mentoring and a synthesis of the literature on military mentoring to ground the narratives from our study in chapter two and three. To expand the academic dialogue and existing programming on mentoring, we outlined the Endarkened Feminist Mentor Program more concretely in chapter 4. We concluded our manuscript with a practical guide for researching with undergraduate scholars using our program and included specific strategies, resources, and writing prompts to assist practitioners in the field.

In this chapter, the ROTC scholars speak to the significance of meeting one of their mentors (Dr. La Vonne I. Neal) for the first time, which underscores the importance of answering the call to a life-changing opportunity. The day they met their mentor at a military ball at Northern Illinois University (NIU) is a crucial moment on their life's path, and a turning point in the development of their scholar identity. Gilman Whiting defines scholar identity as "one in which individuals view themselves as academicians, as studious, as competent and capable, and intelligent."[14] Whiting's Scholar Identity Model (SIM) characterizes scholar identity into nine constructs with each construct grounded in a theory or theories.[15] The eighth and ninth construct of Whiting's SIM model pertains to gender (masculinity) and race (racial identity). So we omitted the ninth construct (masculinity) when helping our female cadets develop scholar identity more fully.

Gilman Whiting's Scholar Identity Model[16]

Fast-forward three years later, the scholars now in key leadership positions in ROTC (e.g. NIU Huskie Cadet Battalion Commander, etc.) and university honor societies (e.g. President and Vice President of Mortar Board Honor Society/NIU Chapter) have ambitions to finish their doctorates and plans to pursue leadership positions at the highest levels in both academia and the military. This was not always the case before they met their mentors.

Answering the Call for Mentorship: Cadets' Reflections

Why did these scholars accept an invitation to be mentored? As part of the self-study phase of our research, the cadets responded to a question that asked them to reflect on the reasons why they volunteered to be mentored. To support the cadets' academic and professional advancement, we conducted participatory action research that required them to be active participants in learning. As a community, we conceptualized a research study titled: "Borders, Bras, and Battles: Sociocultural Perspectives of Female Scholars of Color in ROTC." This action research approach assisted them in identifying borders that may prevent equality in institutions (e.g., academia & military) and how to carve pathways to successfully navigate social justice battles. What follows are excerpts from their self-study interviews.

Personal Narrative (Excerpt from Research Study): Cadet Karina Avila

During my freshman year in ROTC, we had a motivational instructor; Master Sergeant Knight. He was demanding, but the kind of high expectations that made a person want to do something significant with their life at any given time. He extended an invitation to any female in ROTC to be mentored by Dr. La Vonne Neal. In that moment, I had no idea what I was getting myself into, but it sounded like a great opportunity. Two of my battle buddies Maria, Shanell, and I were the only ones to volunteer. What was going to happen next...I could not have ever imagined.

Dr. Neal was one of the guest speakers at our ROTC military ball during my freshman year. I answered the call for mentoring with her because I remembered the ever-lasting impact that her presence had when I first saw her. She walked with elegance and grace, and that alone kept me interested in what she was all about. When she spoke, I paid attention to how successful she was. She did so much from being a track & field star to being a Military Intelligence officer, while still keeping true to her cultural identity. I have looked up to her since that day. Everything she did was inspiring, and that is why I could not pass up the opportunity to learn from her.

I am the proud daughter of parents who migrated to the U.S. from Mexico. My first year in college was difficult to navigate because I am a first-generation college student. I am honored to have the opportunity to attend college thanks to my parents and my end goal is to make them and my younger sister proud. Dr. Neal helped me understand that danger is real and fear is a choice. She believed in me, and that was enough to get me back on track academically without fear.[17]

Personal Narrative (Excerpt from Research Study): Cadet Maria Colompos

Two years ago at our annual military ball, Dr. Neal was asked to present a speech to the NIU Huskie Battalion. She was the Dean of the College of Education at Northern Illinois University and former captain in Military Intelligence in the U.S. Army. I vividly remember her stride to the podium with her stunning black gown. It was as if she floated like an angel to the podium. The first words out of her mouth were compelling enough to make me stop eating, and look directly into her eyes. The way she spoke was truly a work of art: a unique presentation style, intriguing facial and body mannerisms, and a dashing appearance.

After she spoke, I was determined to learn more about her. I was devastated that I was not able to introduce myself personally to her at the military ball. The weekend after the military ball, in my military science class my military instructor, MSG Knight, asked us to raise our hand if we wanted to be mentored by Dr. Neal. I dropped my pen, and raised my hand as high as I could. I was surprised that only two other cadets raised their hands as well. From that moment on, I knew that it was one of the best decisions I have ever made.

There are three main reasons why I chose to answer the call for mentoring. The first is that I was captivated by her confidence. There are very few people in my life that I consider to have a confident presence. She had a powerful voice and I immediately realized that she was the acculturated mother figure that I needed in order to continue my academic career. Also, her voice reminded me of my grandmother because of how genuinely she expressed her visions of the importance of making a difference. Secondly, her speech allowed me to automatically create an unbreakable bond of trust with her because of her initiative to help others achieve greatness. I have heard countless speeches from high achieving professionals, yet only a few of them had a compelling message that resonated with me.

Additionally, out of the few compelling speeches that resonated with me, Dr. Neal was the only one who established a professional brand for herself and accentuated the importance of being a well-rounded leader. Lastly, she made me feel comfortable about who I am. I thought she could potentially help me truly find my purpose in life. Dr. Neal made me feel comfortable and I was able to relate to her because she was a woman who served in the military and one who has held numerous positions of power. Her willingness to motivate and encourage individuals to reach their goals was extensively implied in her speech. Being able to recognize qualities in an individual upon the first meeting like the ones I immediately saw in Dr. Neal is rare. The rareness of my brief encounter with her at the military ball was more than enough ammunition to keep my interest in her.[18]

Personal Narrative (Excerpt from Research Study): Cadet Shanell Walter

There are many reasons why I answered the call for mentoring. Dr. Neal gave a speech that was incredible, extraordinary, and powerful, that left an enduring impact on me. She had accomplished so much, from meeting President Barack Obama to being the first African-American woman at her university to be commissioned an officer. Truly amazing right? I agree!

However the main reason I answered the call for mentoring was not solely because of her speech and her accomplishments but because she looked like me. Her skin color was as deep and brown as mine. She mirrored the image of the African-American women you read about, or heard about in history lectures. The Black women you have always dreamed of meeting because they were rare to come across. The women who made a huge difference for the next generations to come. Women like Maya Angelou—to be in their presence is a blessing itself. I had never been in a room with such a successful, phenomenal, and outstanding African-American woman. I had never been so close to an African-American woman who was as ambitious, driven, and passionate about leaving a legacy as Dr. Neal.

On the evening of my very first military ball it was so astonishing to be in the presence of an African-American woman of such greatness. I wanted to know so much more about her. I wanted to converse with her and know her experiences. I was extremely interested in her journey and how she was able to be where she is now. I needed to know how to overcome any future obstacles and challenges that I may face being a woman, and woman of color in the United States Army.

That very night, my military instructor told me to not let Dr. Neal leave without getting a picture with her. He said this picture would be one of the most significant pictures I would take as an undergraduate and a cadet, but I missed the opportunity to do so. I was very upset with myself; I had let the opportunity of introducing myself to one of the greatest leaders of my time pass me. That night all I could think about was how did I miss that once in a lifetime opportunity?

As a child I would tell my mom that if I were an inventor I would invent a time machine to meet Rosa Parks, Wilma Rudolph, Harriet Tubman, Coretta Scott King, and many others. I always believed women like them were women whom you should want to model and if you ever see them, make it your business to meet them because that moment is just that special. Seeing Dr. Neal and hearing her speak made me passionate and eager to know more about her.

Shortly after the military ball, Dr. Neal extended the invitation to mentor cadets within the Huskie Battalion. That very moment I realized that dreams do come true and God answers prayers. I could not miss another opportunity to meet with Dr. Neal; there was no way I would. I had never had a mentor and was extremely excited when she extended an invitation to mentor us. I knew I could learn so much from her and gain so much knowledge that would help me grow as a phenomenal leader just like her. I knew if I had Dr. Neal as my mentor I would learn how to navigate within the military as a woman of color and become successful. I knew that she would prepare me mentally for the journey ahead. I had no idea how important mentors were and how much they matter.[19]

Summation of Findings: Personal Narratives

Overall, three themes emerged when we analyzed the cadets' self-interviews: (1) success, (2) opportunities, and (3) confidence. The cadets answered the call for mentorship because they were inspired by the way one of their mentors spoke at the military ball about her leadership opportunities. They were impressed by her record of career success, and confident that she could also help them achieve their own career success.

It is also important to note that for Cadet Walter, having a mentor who looked like "the image of the African American women you read about, or heard about in history lectures" made her feel she could overcome any challenges she might face as a woman and woman of color in the United States Army. We will delve more deeply into the importance of having mentors and leaders who look like the people they serve in chapter two, but before we address this important issue, we will pivot to a question readers may have at this point.

Becoming an Ally

What happens if you are a mentor who is culturally, linguistically, and/or ethnically different than your mentee? Does this mean you cannot be an effective mentor? Thankfully, the answer is no; you can be a very effective mentor. You just have to reframe the way you approach the idea, and change the lens you use to envision a mentor program. The important part is to remember to reframe the way you see yourself first; redefine and educate yourself to be an ally—open to seeing yourself and others in new ways.

An ally is "a member of a [privileged] group who rejects the dominant ideology and takes action against oppression out of a belief that eliminating oppression will benefit everyone." [20] You can be a member of any privileged group and take action against oppression. For example, you could be an able-bodied man, (a member of two privileged groups: male and able-bodied) and work as a volunteer with veterans who are physically disabled as an ally to support veterans' rights. As a volunteer who works with veterans, you are volunteering in the spirit of solidarity to improve the quality of the veterans' lives. It is important to reframe the way you see yourself as a member of certain privileged groups. For example, if you are able-bodied, you should reframe the way you see your status as temporarily able-bodied because you too could become injured in the workplace or in a car collision and become physically disabled at any given time. The most important piece to remember when becoming an ally is to approach allyship from a state of action where you continuously work to disrupt and dismantle systems of oppression in solidarity with members of marginalized groups. You enter allyship to engage the learning process. In other words, you do not become an ally to seek credit for your actions or receive praise for your work, or to speak on behalf of any member of a marginalized group. You become an ally because you genuinely believe that your liberation is connected to the liberation of others. As Audre Lorde once said, "I am not free while any woman is unfree, even when her shackles are very different than my own."[21]

While membership to certain privileged groups is more permanent (such as being white or heterosexual), there are always varying degrees of horizontal oppression working within those groups. As Rita Hardiman and Bailey Jackson write:

> Horizontal oppression is also at work when members of privileged groups physically attack, criticize, or ostracize other group members who work with [people who are culturally, linguistically, and ethnically diverse] to dismantle oppression, for example, when white people who challenge racism are called racial slurs or when the sexuality of heterosexual people who challenge heterosexism is questioned.[22]

When you decide to engage in allyship, it is vital to start recognizing how oppression operates in multidimensional ways and on various fronts—environmental, institutional, societal, and individual.[23] This can be difficult at first because we all have been socialized since birth (through pop culture, the media, various institutions such as work, and school) to accept systems of oppression as normal.[24]

In the case of a mentorship relationship, you are an ally who has decided to actively work against oppression such as ableism, racism, sexism, linguicism, ageism, heterosexism, and xenophobia through your professional work. What does this look like as a mentor? We have a specific mentor program that delves more deeply into the details in chapters 4 & 5. However, the essence of being an ally means that you honor the cultural, linguistic, ethnic, and spiritual roots that each person brings to the table. These differences must be viewed as strengths and not deficits.

Rubin A. Gastambid-Fernandez writes compellingly about the creative solidarity that is forged through this work—when our mentees' differences become a source of strength that draws us closer together. He posits:

> [This work] also requires a redefinition of how we go
> about relating to others and how we choose to engage
> others in an attempt to, on the one hand, recognize
> their difference from ourselves, while on the other,
> build bonds that transgress the very boundaries that
> such recognition of difference crystallizes.[25]

It is when we transgress our differences through building bonds, our mentees sense these new bonds through the genuine warmth of our interactions, our affect, and our actions. In our mentoring sessions, these bonds are also strengthened through storytelling about life experiences (e.g., navigating military, academic, personal, and leadership challenges), sharing culturally relevant music, celebrating mentees' individual and collective accomplishments, and listening to individual and group struggles.

CHAPTER 2

Academic Perspectives on Mentoring

A Synthesis of Undergraduate Mentoring Research Meta Analyses from 1970s to 2015

To establish academic support that would sustain the cadets as they expanded their knowledge of research processes, the scholars took several research courses at NIU— independent study courses taught by Sarah Militz-Frielink. As part of the initial research course, the cadets began an exploration of their own personal and collective reflections on systems of inequality in academia and in the military, communities of resistance, and on the framework for their mentorship relationships – the Endarkened Feminist Epistemology. The following was accomplished through the completion of the course requirements:

1. Institutional Review Board (IRB) training;
2. Co-authored research proposal: "Borders, Bras, and Battles: Sociocultural Perspectives of Female Scholars of Color in ROTC;"
3. Synthesis of related literature and written literature reviews;
4. Conducted self-study interviews and qualitative interviews; and coded the results;
5. Co-authored a research paper highlighting the findings of

Phase 1 of the study;

6. Co-presented with their mentors the research paper at the following four conferences:

- The 99th Annual Association for the Study of African American Life and History (ASALH) Convention in Memphis, Tennessee. The ASALH convention is an international conference that features researchers from around the world who study Black life, history, and culture.

- The 22nd Annual National Character and Leadership Symposium (NCLS) at the United States Air Force Academy (USAFA) at Colorado Springs, CO. This symposium is one of the premier national symposiums in the field of character and leadership development. We were invited as presenters.

- The 2015 NIU Undergraduate Research and Artistry Conference, Dekalb, IL

- The 2015 National Conference of the Association of Black Women in Higher Education (ABWHE) at Chicago, IL. The ABWHE has five chapters nationwide and the conference has served as a forum for developing strategies to improve the quality of education of Black people with a commitment to aiding Black women in the academy in fulfilling their own aspirations.

- Co-authored a chapter for an edited book.

- Co-authored a proposal to present a paper at the 25th Annual National Association for Multicultural Education (NAME) Conference. The proposal was accepted.

- Co-authored an academic journal article—"Leadership Through Knowledge: U.S. Army ROTC Cadets' Sojourn Through African American History and Military Legacies;" Academic Journal: *The Black History Bulletin*, a peer-reviewed academic journal was established in 1937 by Dr. Carter G. Woodson to inform the knowledge base for the professional praxis of secondary educators and teacher educators.

• Co-authored a book.

The scholars accomplished all of this while simultaneously completing their military duties and degree specific academic work—often taking 18-21 credit hours a semester. How did we motivate our scholars to accomplish all of this? Three words: Endarkened Feminist Epistemology! Before we describe our mentor program, we pause to take a look at the literature published on undergraduate mentoring programs over the past 40 years that helped us grasp a better contextual understanding of mentoring, what works, and does not work, what needs to change in undergraduate programs to be more successful. This chapter also contains the perspectives of Regina A. Lewis, Ph.D.; one of our research participants, a Gulf War veteran and accomplished academic.

Mentoring Programs from 1970s to Today: An Academic Perspective

Since the late 1970s, there has been a plethora of literature published on the importance of mentoring programs and relationships in various academic disciplines from education and psychology to health care and business. While the operational definitions of mentoring, and the theories used to frame studies about mentoring, have typically varied, researchers have generally come to a consensus that mentoring involves the growth and accomplishment of an individual, a career and of personal and professional development through a mentor/mentee relationship that involves role modeling and social support. However, during the literature review on academic and military mentoring relationships and programs for scholars who are CLED, it became clear that while there is some consensus on the definition of "mentoring", there are definitely inconsistencies related to which research methodologies are held as valid when used to examine mentoring this population.

For this study, we selected the work of Maryann Jacobi as the most salient framework for examining mentoring relationships for students and women who CLED. Since 1991, there have been three critical reviews of mentoring research published, along with its related literature.[26] [27] [28]

Maryann Jacobi conducted the first critical analysis of undergraduate mentoring programs and found three key weaknesses in mentoring studies: (1) a lack of a clear or agreed upon definition of mentoring, (2) weaknesses in theoretical frameworks to support mentoring research, (3) and flaws in methodologies.[29] Despite these inconsistencies, the majority of studies have suggested that there is an indirect relationship between mentoring and academic or career success.

Mentoring has often been recommended as a means of providing women and people who are CLED with the support, socialization, and assistance they need to succeed in an environment they may experience as alienating or even hostile.[30] Thus women and people who are CLED may seek "mentors of the same gender and ethnicity, and may experience difficulty in relating to or learning from mentors of a different gender or ethnicity."[31] Jacobi's review of the literature revealed that mentors of the same ethnic background as their mentees can assist in helping students resolve conflicts between the values of one's cultural background and the values of the institution.[32] Furthermore, mentors of the same ethnicity can teach mentees that success is possible without abandoning one's cultural identity.[33] Research has also demonstrated that having a mentor is one of the most important experiences for women who are CLED who want to pursue careers in academia.[34] Dr. Regina A. Lewis, one of our research study participants (U.S. Air Force & Gulf War veteran) and mentee of one the authors, spoke to this phenomenon as she reflected on her experiences being a doctoral scholar.

> Obtaining a Ph.D. was an implausible idea for me. There were many concerns that tainted my belief that I would be able to achieve this level of education.

Working full-time and being a single parent did not leave much room to pursue a doctorate. Yet, Dr. Neal, who was the Dean of the College of Education, led the development of a cohort-based doctoral program for working adults with extended obligations.[35]

Throughout the literature, researchers have surprisingly noted that the majority of mentoring studies have been underdeveloped and fraught with flaws in validity. Despite these weaknesses, the value of mentoring has long been accepted in the literature as well as in practice.[36] Most notably, it appears that mentoring research has made little progress in the identification, development and conceptualization of mentoring. Hence there is a need for a practical guide that includes the specifics of a mentoring relationship with undergraduates, the full conceptualization of how research is conducted with undergraduates, and the identification of a more comprehensive mentor program, which we illuminate further in the subsequent chapters.

A 2015 study on mentorship which examined the experiences of 58 faculty of color at 22 tier 1 research institutions generated three main themes: (a) life course practices geared toward accumulating social capital are critical; (b) major barriers are linked to the undervaluing of faculty research areas and community-engaged scholarly commitments; and (c) connections with mentors who understand the struggles specific to faculty of color can assist with retention and success in predominantly white institutions.[37] Using the findings of this 2015 study as one of the foundations of our research guide, we have built upon these themes and explored these issues in practice with undergraduate researchers (see chapter 5).

Similar themes have been present in the literature about "other mothering" and "community and cultural connections" among teachers and successful children of color in schools.[38] African-American women and teachers have actively played the role of "mother" to the children of others since the heinous era of slavery when it was considered to be a responsibility, especially of teachers, to make sure that children were safe from harm. Though times have changed, some teachers and mentors still find that the role of other mother is a significant part of their responsibilities. In our study, all three scholars expressed the impact of other mothering. Cadet Avila's narratives revealed the other mothering theme through Dr. Neal's concern for her family: "Dr. Neal always asked about our families and keeps them informed about our success. She always showed concern for them, which is something not many people do. It showed us that she cared for us not only as her mentees, but almost like daughters that she took under her wing."[39]

Likewise, in one of Cadet Colompos' narratives, she associates Dr. Neal's voice with her grandmother: "She had a powerful voice and I immediately realized that she was the acculturated mother figure that I needed in order to continue my academic career. Also, her voice reminded me of my grandmother because of how genuinely she expressed her visions of the importance of making a difference."[40]

Like a daughter, Cadet Walter took advice from Dr. Neal on relationship matters. "She has given me motherly guidance about young men, and one thing I could never forget her saying is 'You are a scholar; I suggest you date a scholar, someone who compliments you.'"[41]

Research on effective African-American teachers has shown that they rely on strong ties to their community and culture and those ties were used to make culturally relevant, positive connections about school and education for all students of color.[42] Like our community of caring, many cultures have similar cultural connections, and these connections were used to create positive expectations of our mentees' academic experiences.

Since Jacobi's comprehensive review of mentoring literature in 1991, Crisp and Cruz have reviewed 42 empirical studies spanning the years 1990 through 2007. They discovered that since the 1990s, more mentoring studies have been published with an emphasis on marginalized groups. However, Crisp and Cruz also noticed a gap in the types of theoretical frameworks used to study underrepresented groups and "recommended that [mentoring] theory expand to include underpinnings of critical race and feminist theories as well as theories from other fields."[43]

We took note of this gap and expanded the framing of our scholarship to include the blending of several theories, most notably Endarkened Feminist Theory, but also Post-Colonial and Critical Race Theory.[44] Like Jacobi, the critical review conducted by Crisp and Cruz over a 17-year-period of time, which also included literature from psychology and business, revealed the need for a better understanding of mentoring programs, especially the characteristics of the participants. While general findings have been pointing to the positive impact mentoring has on student persistence or grade point average, the gap in studying the characteristics of mentees is still present in the literature. Thus, some of the main questions in the Borders, Bras, and Battles self-study questionnaire were used to assess the unique characteristics of undergraduate participants in our mentoring program.

Gershenfeld's 2008 - 2012 critical review of undergraduate mentoring programs, found that overall progress has been made with respect to the use of theory or conceptual frameworks. The critical review findings also indicated that "a single guiding theory would be inappropriate given the range of outcomes measured in undergraduate mentoring programs."[45] Gershenfeld's review also noted that undergraduate mentoring programs generally serve more than one function and those that are implemented with the highest frequency are programs that include academic support, psychosocial support, and role modeling[46] – all hallmarks of good mentoring programs. These study findings are in line with the design of our program.

Gershenfeld also discovered another salient mentoring theme that has appeared in a limited number of studies—goal setting and helping with career paths—which also happens to be a critical component of our program (and is further elaborated on in chapter 5). While it is crucial to remember that not all undergraduate mentoring programs are the same, Gershenfeld's critical review emphasized that "key operational features of mentoring programs must be specified including characteristics of mentors/mentees, functions of mentoring role, mentor-mentee ratio, frequency and duration of mentoring meetings, expected duration of mentoring commitment, types and extent of training and other support as well as whether the program is mandatory or voluntary." [47]

In the following reflection, Dr. Regina A. Lewis delves into her mentor's characteristics, the supports and impact having a mentor during her Ph.D. program made on her overall progress as a leader.

Research Participant Reflection (Excerpt from Study): Dr. Regina A. Lewis

I was a member of a doctoral program cohort at the University of Colorado at Colorado Springs and Dr. Neal was our biggest cheerleader. She continuously visited with us in the classroom and one on one. I can still hear her say, there is no reason why you cannot graduate in 3 years if you want to and you will graduate if you collaborate. Her words were always memorable. To help me through the program, Dr. Neal would always reference / cite researchers during our discussions. It always amazed me that no matter what I was talking about she would magically go to her "wonder" files and not only pull materials that complemented or reinforced what I was working on, but the article or book would be tabbed. Her years of research and work along with her impeccable organization demonstrated her life-long focus and attention to detail.

It wasn't just Dr. Neal's words of encouragement that was the core of my achievement, but her ability to speak to my strengths that allowed me to keep going even when I wanted to give up. Dr. Neal never told me what to do or pointed out where I was wrong, instead, she had a special way of giving me extremely important advice and leaving it open for me to decide by saying You may want to consider or I cannot speak for anyone else, this has been my experience.

Through it all, Dr. Neal was a strong supporter for all of us and I consider her a transformational and authentic leader which helped shape me to be the scholar I am today—a university professor and department chairperson.[48]

CHAPTER 3
U.S. Military Perspectives on Mentoring

A Synthesis of Military Mentoring Research, Regulations and Programs

The very first mentor in Western civilization appeared in Homer's *Odyssey*. Odysseus considered Mentor a dear friend and entrusted him with the teaching and caring of his son, Telemachus, while Odysseus fought in the Trojan War. Yet, most of Telemachus' guidance came from Athena, the goddess of wisdom, who was also the warrior goddess. Athena frequently came to Telemachus disguised as Mentor. "Thus the very first alternative mentoring occurred within a military setting, and that alternative mentor was a woman."[49] The historical presence of a woman as one of the first mentors in a military setting has significant implications for the work we are doing in *Borders, Bras, and Battles*.

In Greek mythology, Athena, was not only portrayed as a mentor and a warrior goddess, but the "embodiment of wisdom, reason, and purity."[50] As an example, she is also credited with several inventions: the bridle, the trumpet, the flute, the pot, the rake, the plow, the yoke, the ship, and the chariot.[51] Her role as a woman serving in combat arms was never questioned as she fought in battles defending her home and her state against enemies. It is in the spirit of Athena that we delve into the literature about mentoring in the military, focusing on mentoring that supports intellectual growth and personal and professional development. Interwoven throughout the literature, will be the voices of some of the "Athena's" from today, *Borders, Bras, and Battles* research participants: Dr. Regina A. Lewis (U.S. Air Force / Gulf War veteran; University Professor), and Colonel Gail Colvin (retired) (U.S. Air Force Academy graduate / 1st cohort of women; Administrator at the U.S. Air Force Academy)—who will share what it is like to lead and to be led, to mentor and to be mentored, to be role models for women in academia, in the military, and the world today.

While there is a wide-range of interpretations of mentoring among the military branches, the overwhelming majority of mentoring studies have consistently revealed that mentoring had significant positive correlations with work performance, personal health, quality of interpersonal relationships, greater career recognition, and general career competence.[52] The following paragraphs examine the pros and cons of military mentoring programs and were used to identify challenges and to extract components of those practices deemed to be useful in supplementing the Endarkened Feminist Mentor Program that we developed.

U.S. Air Force Mentoring Program: A Fundamental Responsibility

The U.S. Air Force (USAF) mandates mentoring in U.S. Air Force Institution (AFI) 36-3401, Air Force Mentoring. According to AFI 36-3401, mentoring is a "relationship in which a person with greater experience and wisdom [the mentor] guides another person [the subordinate] to develop both personally and professionally."[53] In response, the USAF has had the following formal instructions on mentoring since 1996: "Mentoring is a fundamental responsibility of all Air Force supervisors. They must know their people, accept personal responsibility for them, and be accountable for their professional development."[54] However, because of a myriad of reasons, research shows that this is not as simple as the statement infers.

One study from a professional military education program revealed that "Air Force mentoring programs substitute career building for leadership development, which distracts leaders from maximizing the leadership potential of Air Force personnel."[55] The results suggested that mentoring programs that focus on building airmen's leadership skills would greatly benefit the Air Force. Another qualitative study revealed tensions between baby boomer mentors and their (Gen X) mentees. For example, one USAF core value is "Service before Self," which boomers often translate as stay as late as needed to finish the job. This seems to be in direct contrast with some Gen-X mentees who value a work-life balance, and "in their own words, seek to 'have a life' beyond the military."[56] Paradoxically, it was found that this generational difference led to a quandary in the mentoring relationship—how to deal with conflict, especially between mentees and their mentors.[57]

Despite the documented complexities of mentoring relationships involving generational differences, our study pointed to the importance of having same sex role models in the military. Colonel Gail Colvin speaks to the impact role models had on her experiences at the United States Air Force Academy (USAFA) as one of the first women and African American women admitted into the academy (class of 1980).

> There was such a strong camaraderie among the women in the class of 1980, and there was a social support system intact as the USAFA did an excellent job making sure there were women in our classrooms as instructors, and making sure female role models were as visible as possible. For example, USAFA made sure the role models were trained before our class arrived. Having role models was key in making it more attainable for us to succeed. [58]

U.S. Army Mentoring Program

The U.S. Army Field Manual (FM) 22-100 *Army Leadership* defines mentoring and uses it extensively. FM 22-100 states that mentoring "is the proactive development of each subordinate through observing, assessing, coaching, teaching, developmental counseling, and evaluating that results in people being treated with fairness and equal opportunity"[59]

Gregg Martin, George Reed, Ruth Collins, and Cortez Dial conducted a study in 2002 on mentoring experiences in the Army, which revealed that 91 percent of military officers attending the National War College (in a sample of 305 senior officers) had been mentored during their military careers and that 87 percent had mentored other military members in turn. They reported benefits from both career and psychosocial mentoring functions or mentor behaviors.[60] The U.S. Army had a 2002 survey which included input from nearly 14,000 officers, NCOs, and civilians. Specifically regarding mentoring, the report titled *The Army Training and Leader Development Panel Officer Study Report to the Army* concluded:

Officers believe mentoring is important for both personal and professional development, yet a majority of officers report not having mentors. The Army's mentoring definition and doctrine need revising. Officers would like to see a greater emphasis on mentoring, but do not want formal, directed programs.[61]

Despite the resistance to formal programming, mentoring has also been associated with long-term commitment and satisfaction within the Army. For example, a longitudinal study with over 1,000 U.S. Army Officers revealed that mentored Army employees had higher levels of affective commitment and continuance commitment when compared to non-mentored employees one year later. "Thus mentoring may actually contribute to higher levels of affective and continuance commitment to an organization."[62]

U.S. Marine Corps Mentoring Program

The Marine Corps has taken a voluntary approach to mentoring programs. In 1995, the then Commandant General Carl E. Mundy, Jr. ordered commanders to develop voluntary, informal mentoring programs that give all officers opportunities to benefit from mentoring. In an attempt to provide surrogate mentors to enlistees, the Marines have also relied on unit supervisors to meet with recruits after basic training to help them transition to their assignment to a combat unit.[63] "They discuss what has transpired, share their own experiences, give feedback on performance, and discuss their future positions in the unit."[64] Nevertheless, there have been documented issues in finding mentors for female Marines.

A 2012 study conducted by Emerald M. Archer at Woodbury University, suggested that gender-role stereotypes influence opportunities for female marine mentorship, and that "most female officers noted that there is little to no mentorship for female officers specifically or female marines generally.[65] Even though Archer's study also showed that male marines can serve as role models and mentors for female marines, many male marines are reluctant to take on this role because they might be accused of giving special attention to a female marine.[66]

Dr. Regina A. Lewis believes that recruiting and retaining more women of color may help alleviate situations where female officers lack mentors in the military. "We need more women of color at the decision-making table of the military," she said during the research interview. "This means our young women scholars need to set their goals high and enter the military at a leadership level. In other words we need young women to become officers, go through ROTC, or the military academies. We need role models and mentors who can pave the way and also place others on the path and guide them."[67]

U.S. Navy Mentoring Program

The Navy is known for its emphasis on the development of a specialty advisor who provides specialty guidance for career development.

This leader is a senior individual who is appointed to serve as an intermediary among four constituencies: "the individual, specialty corps, the Navy community, and the detailer (or job assignment officer).[68] The specialty leader may act as a lobbyist or liaison in personnel matters, assist the detailer in assigning jobs, and act as an advisor to individuals.

In a recent military study, 568 midshipmen at the United States Naval Academy (USNA) responded to a survey regarding their experience of having been mentored at USNA. Results indicated that 45% of midshipmen are mentored and that women are more likely to have a mentor (63%) than men (42%). The study also revealed that "mentored midshipmen (who included both male and female officers) who were significantly more satisfied with United States Naval Academy, viewed mentorships as more important, and were more active mentors themselves.[69] Overall, USNA midshipmen who were mentored were more likely to find value in mentorships, reported increased self-esteem, and opportunities as a result of the mentoring relationship.[70]

Summation of Military Mentoring

The review on mentoring has resulted in positive themes throughout the branches of the military especially in the following areas: (1) high self-esteem; (2) increased career opportunities; and (3) psychosocial support.

Research Participant Reflection (Excerpt from Study): Colonel Gail Colvin (retired)

Although Colonel Gail Colvin had excellent female role models at the United States Air Force Academy, she did not always have opportunities to be mentored by females after graduation. Colonel Colvin reflected upon her experiences being the only woman and woman of color during the first part of her military career. Lacking female role models and mentoring opportunities, Colonel Colvin attributes her high levels of performance as the primary way she dealt with gender and race challenges during the first half of her career. "The better I performed the more confident I became about being a woman and being of color. For the first half of my career, I was the only woman and only person of color in my work setting, so I held back my unique perspectives at work until I realized that my perspectives were valid and were absolutely what my superiors needed to hear."[71]

Colonel Colvin explained that she eventually learned to reach out, collaborate with other colleagues, and recognize how valuable her perspectives really were to her superiors.

> This is where I lacked a skill set, since I was used to working in isolation, doing more than my share of work, and having such a competent reputation. Yet, I needed to learn how to collaborate, and how to build relationships with other influencers. I needed to personalize myself with other people, which surprisingly cut down my workload as we shared responsibilities. When you can relate with people on another level, you will get considered for other positions.[72]

When asked about mentoring and what an ideal mentor should be like, Colonel Colvin summed up her thoughts on the topic:

> When I think of a mentor, I think back to a person who can teach you the unwritten rules, and the extra ways to prepare yourself. You need someone to help guide you. Sometimes it is having someone to help you, to guide you, and mentor you that makes all the difference in excelling in a new job or academic program.[73]

Colonel Colvin also said that mentoring in the military should be reexamined especially with respect to retention. She stated that although the military has made great strides toward equality for all people, it still has more progress to make. She explained:

> To be specific, the military needs to rethink how to sustain retention in leadership positions, especially

leadership positions women and people of color occupy. The military could also benefit from rethinking how to appeal to women who are culturally, linguistically, and/or ethnically diverse. Questions such as: What makes someone stay in the military? What is their day-to-day experience? How are they being valued? How do you not marginalize them? How are you making them feel comfortable? should be re-visited. [74]

CHAPTER 4
A Community of Caring:
Endarkened Feminist Mentorship

Our "Endarkened Feminist Mentor Program," is a community of caring including three mentors from three different universities and three U.S. Army ROTC female cadets / scholars who are culturally, linguistically, and/or ethnically diverse. What distinguishes our work from traditional mentorship programs is that we use a transnational endarkened feminist epistemological paradigm to ground our mentoring sessions and research courses.

Transnational endarkened feminist epistemology is primarily a research paradigm and teaching framework created by multiculturalist, Cynthia B. Dillard, the Mary Frances Early Professor of Education at the University of Georgia in the department of Educational Theory and Practice. As the chief architect of this paradigm, Dillard drew upon the strengths of four feminist and/or spiritual frameworks to create her epistemology. These frameworks include: (1) black feminist thought, the work of Patricia Hill-Collins; (2) standpoint theory, the work of Sandra Harding; (3) the tenets of African American spirituality; and (4) non-religious spirituality in education—the work of Parker J. Palmer.[75]

According to Dillard, Endarkened feminist epistemology is used to:

Articulate how reality is known when based in the historical roots of Black feminist thought, embodying a distinguishable difference in cultural standpoint, located in the intersection/overlap of the culturally constructed socializations of race, gender, and other identities, and the historical and contemporary contexts of oppressions and resistance for African American women.[76]

Using a humanist/modernist approach, Dillard has constructed endarkened feminist epistemology as an alternative paradigm to the "Big Four" research frameworks: (1) positivism, (2) post-positivism, (3) critical theory, and (4) constructivism. She rejects the big four as absolute and the assumption that researchers need to align with one of them as their "Big Daddy protector."[77] We believe this is one of the primary strengths of her framework because it provides alternative ways of positioning one's self as a scholar in the academy—especially for researchers who may not identify with traditional ways of thinking or being.

For our undergraduate scholars, mentorship and research approached from an endarkened feminist lens enables them to stay true to their spiritual and cultural roots while honoring their unique traits, histories, and differences as social beings. We subscribe to one of the most salient underpinnings of endarkened feminism, "Different does not mean deficit." This premise works effectively in mentor/mentee relationships as a foundation for empowerment—reframing differences as strengths and encouraging researchers to create new ways of thinking, knowing and being. As a result, researchers learn how to approach research from a different lens and to question commonly accepted notions of truth about the human condition. One way we connect with our mentees as cultural beings is through the use of culturally relevant music, poetry, literature, and art. For example, we play music during our mentor sessions that engage our scholars and reinforce concepts that we discuss such as persistence and resilience. Additionally, we customized music playlists for writing assignments, research, and/or ROTC activities. Below Cadet Shanell Walter shared an instance of how the endarkened feminist mentor model (that includes music) has had a positive impact on her persistence as a social/cultural being.

Personal Narrative (Excerpt from research study): Shanell Walter

Dr. Neal played a song by Ledisi, an incredible artist, titled "Pieces of Me." Throughout this song, Ledisi sings: 'People just don't know what I'm about,.... They haven't seen what's there behind my smile ... There is so much of me I'm showing out...'[78] I feel like Ledisi is singing my story. Others who think I am a certain way because of my skin color—often mischaracterize me. They perceive me to be a certain way because of their misperception of all African Americans, which puts me at an unfair disadvantage. I did not understand this at first; I did not understand why people in academia and the military just could not see me for me—who I am. Yes, I have been through pain, but that is not who I am anymore. I am no longer broken; I have been given another chance to broaden my horizons and make a difference for generations to come after me—every little piece of me. Love and pain consolidates and makes me who I am. My skin color is a part of me, which makes me unique. My naturally textured hair is who I am; it is a piece of me.[79]

Walter's personal message is also a communal message. It embodies the spirit of what Gist communicated when she powerfully referenced Harris-Perry[80] in her foreword. Harris-Perry described a type of crooked room phenomenon based on field dependence studies where people adjust their physical positioning based on their perceptions of the surrounding environment. Walter brings Harris-Perry's argument alive as her experiences point to the fact that Black women often experience society as a crooked room of stereotypes and manipulations telling them to align with harmful images and practices around them.

Despite perceiving and experiencing this context, women from marginalized communities must find pathways and tools to see themselves as possessing unrestricted potentialities that neutralize the potency of these crippling paradigms. Subsequently, we designed a tool—a playlist for the scholars to remind them of their unrestricted potential. Music from the playlist includes: (1) "Pieces of Me" by Ledisi; (2) "It's My Time" by Kelly Price; (3) "Conqueror" by Estelle; (4) "Doubt" by Mary J. Blige.

Cadet Karina Avila writes about how this tool helped unleash her potential through the endarkened feminist mentor program: "I will not doubt myself anymore, and I know Dr. Neal will reassure me of that. I thank god for her mentorship every day. Like Mary J. Blige says 'I'm gonna be the best me, Sorry if it kills you!'"[81] We see endarkened feminist epistemology as a pathway to creative solidarity.

The Research Process as an Ideological Undertaking

Cynthia B. Dillard gives credit for the endarkened feminist epistemological approach to the fields of cultural, ethnic and gender studies as these academic disciplines have challenged traditional epistemological biases and underpinnings in the research process.[82] Traditional research paradigms such as positivism do not recognize the research process as an ideological undertaking—one that is deeply embedded within the viewpoints, cultural understandings, and discourse style of the researcher. Epistemological racism means that our current range of research epistemologies—positivism to postmodernism/post structuralisms—arise out of the social history and culture of the dominant race. These epistemologies reflect and reinforce the social history of the dominant racial group (while excluding the epistemologies of other races/cultures). This has negative results for people who are CLED.[83]

Racial critiques of research epistemologies have virtually nothing to do with whether an individual researcher is overtly or covertly racist. A researcher could be adamantly anti-racist in thought and deed and still be using a research epistemology that…could be judged to be racially biased.[84]

When we ask questions about, acknowledge, and connect with the sociocultural viewpoints, understandings, and histories of our mentees, we have noted that, in response, the cadets/scholars rise and overcome any academic challenge.

Framing our Research Questions in the Study

When we first started deliberating about our research project with our scholars, we also examined our research questions from a critical race and post-colonial theoretical framework. The critical race and post-colonial theoretical framework was used as a lens to examine the very essence of the reasons why women of color and/or multiple ethnicities choose to pursue simultaneous careers in academia and the military and what social, historical, and cultural factors contribute to their decision to pursue these dual missions. We also wanted to know how ROTC cadets have negotiated various race, ethnicity, and gender challenges during their time in the military and academia as well as what is needed in the military and in academia to recruit and retain more women who are culturally, linguistically, or ethnically diverse.

The Literature Search

When we examined the literature in Gender Studies and Military Science, we found that there is a paucity of research on women who are CLED in ROTC. Nevertheless the themes that kept reappearing in the literature are policies—Army Regulation (AR) 600-20 (which addresses equal treatment and language)[85] and Army Regulation (AR) 670-1 (addresses hair and dress codes).[86] AR 600-20 is written to provide an environment free of unlawful discrimination and offensive behavior, members of marginalized groups can expect fair treatment and have legal recourse if that is not the case. This policy is a factor that helps attract women who are CLED to ROTC and helps them feel more confident when dealing with race or gender challenges.

Conversely, AR 670-1 poses economic, race and gender-related challenges as it bans dreadlocks, twists, or any bulk of hair that exceeds two inches from the scalp. This policy may create challenges for women who are CLED that have naturally textured hair since in order to abide by it they have to spend a lot of money on hair relaxers, which can set them further back economically from their white counterparts. This is also challenging at the cultural level because some women who are CLED may prefer to keep their hair in a natural state.

We also found that Army Regulation 600-20, can pose cultural and social challenges for women who are linguistically diverse. Since English is required while performing military functions, women who are linguistically diverse have to work harder to protect their linguistic roots by finding and maintaining friendships with other women who are linguistically diverse in the army. Personal conversations in the army are not regulated, which helps women who are linguistically diverse forge those bonds and maintain language fluency.

Motivational Factors for Accomplishing Tasks

Our cadets/scholars conducted an ambitious research project while successfully completing their military duties, academic obligations in their degree programs, extra-curricular activities, volunteer service, and family obligations. We believe the endarkened feminist mentorship/research model, which helped frame not only our research study questions, but also our research meetings and coaching sessions, inspired our scholars to perform at high academic levels. For example, the literature review, and the research questions, were directly linked to the cadets' experiences in ROTC as women who are culturally, linguistically, and ethnically diverse. The army regulations we studied and analyzed from an endarkened feminist lens were the same army regulations that our cadets had to abide by in ROTC. As researchers, the cadets were thinking critically—questioning commonly accepted notions of truth and about the human condition.

The research questions, which we used to create the self-interview questionnaires, that the cadets filled out themselves and coded, were relevant to their current experiences, perspectives, ambitions, and goals as women who are culturally, linguistically, and ethnically diverse pursuing dual missions in academia and the military. The interview questions, which we also posed to female military veterans who also had careers in academia, were of high interest to our undergraduate researchers because the results would provide insights about being a woman and a leader who is CLED in the military.

In summary, the relevance of the research study questions as they were directly related to our undergraduates' lives and future careers was one of the most salient motivation factors in this project. The particular design and relevancy of this study could not have been possible without Cynthia B. Dillard's endarkened feminist epistemological paradigm.

Endarkened Feminist Mentorship in Action

The following excerpts include qualitative and quantitative data to illustrate the impact Endarkened Feminist Mentorship has had on our scholars over the past three years. We begin with three vignettes where the scholars share how mentoring has positively changed their academic and personal lives, and then conclude with numbers to show the collective increase in academic performance and service in the community.

Karina Avila

"You said I'd never be a leader, you said I'd never wear a crown, If I wanted to be someone, I should learn to settle down" sings Mary J. Blige in her song "Doubt" with emotion. Things like that are what I heard all of the time, whether it was from other people, or me constantly doubting myself. One thing, I can say without a doubt is that I never heard anything like this from Dr. Neal, and she helped me not doubt myself. Dr. Neal came into my life at the perfect time! It's crazy to think that my best friends and I have been working with her for three years now. Within those three years, I have grown tremendously. I have evolved in academics, life, and my career. All of the lessons that I have learned from Dr. Neal, are ones that I will carry with me wherever life decides to take me, and I will use them to help others as well.

As I sit here writing this narrative, I smile. I smile because when I first met with Dr. Neal, my grades were not ideal, and now I can proudly say that I have had the best grades I have ever had. The endless opportunities that Dr. Neal has given me are amazing. From writing publications, to enhancing my public speaking skills by presenting at conferences. The first conference we went to was the Association for the Study of African American Life and History (ASALH), and at first I was very nervous but a part of me knew that we were well prepared. My public speaking skills have improved in classes simply by having the opportunity to present at conferences. I feel more confident, and now I always volunteer to go first in class. The second time we presented was at the U.S. Air Force Academy, and I can honestly say that I had more fun presenting there because I told myself "Hey, this isn't your first rodeo" and I was less nervous. Plus, seeing the way Dr. Neal presents and captivates the audience is amazing, and I know someday I will have those skills. We have had the chance to write three publications, it hasn't felt like we have accomplished that much. The other day during one of her mentoring sessions, she read to us part of an article that we wrote, and I was speechless. I was speechless, because I remember sitting at the table, kind of how I am now, writing the first sentence to that article. Therefore, hearing it and seeing it in print just had me in awe. I truly don't know how I will ever thank Dr. Neal enough for all of the encouragement she has provided. The mentorship sessions enhance my focus and help me stay on the right path, and I will forever be grateful.

Life is always one wild rollercoaster, but Dr. Neal has helped ease the turbulence of that rollercoaster. During our mentoring sessions, we discussed personal economics. Learning about how to save and invest money has been great. I now have a wealth management plan to provide for my family. My family has always been my everything, and Dr. Neal always asked about our families and keeps them informed about our success. She always showed concern for them, which is something not many people do. It showed us that she cared for us not only as her mentees, but almost like daughters that she took under her wing.

Throughout those three years, my family and I have become a lot closer. I also just recently got married to the love of my life. Anytime Dr. Neal would talk about economics or our family, I would go straight to my boyfriend (at the time), and tell him all about how we can better our lives. I know he took mental notes, because he has saved more money than ever, and he always asks me to ask Dr. Neal for advice on certain things. My little sister is a big part of my life as well and I hope to be as much of a mentor that Dr. Neal has been to me, to her. I try to teach her everything I know, and now she brings home straight A's and her teachers always have amazing things to say about her. I could not be happier by the way things have turned out with my family.

My career has always been important to me, and it always will be. I had goals growing up of what I wanted to be, and I still have similar goals. Have my goals changed throughout the years? Of course, but only because I have realized what kind of things I enjoy doing. I always thought I would be a nurse, but that quickly changed. I changed my major to rehabilitation services when I realized I enjoyed helping people with disabilities. My goal is to receive a Ph.D. in rehabilitation counseling, and I realized that I wanted to do that within the three years that I have been meeting with Dr. Neal. I never thought I would receive a Ph.D., or that I could even get that far, but after Dr. Neal's mentoring I know that it's possible. She set up a meeting for me with the department chair of the counseling program at NIU. I was able to find out how to get admitted to the program, and what I could do to enhance my chances of getting in. Not many students get that opportunity so I took full advantage of that.

Dr. Neal relates to us in many ways. She was once in the military as well, so she knows exactly what that's like. She believes that all three of us will make it to the U.S. Army Command and General Staff College someday; I don't see why we wouldn't. Dr. Neal is always just a phone call away whenever we have questions about our career and the military, which is really helpful, and eases that crazy rollercoaster called Life.

Now that I am in my senior year of college, I've almost made it. There is a verse in Mary J. Blige's song "Doubt" that says; "I made it to the end, I nearly paid the cost, I lost a lot of friends, I sacrificed a lot, I'd do all again, Cause I made it to the top, But I can't keep doubting myself anymore"[87] That verse could not be said any better. Along the way, I have sacrificed a lot and lost a lot of friends, but I would do it all again in a heartbeat.

Everything I have been through has brought me to where I am today. I would not be where I am today without Dr. Neal. I will not doubt myself anymore, and I know Dr. Neal will reassure me of that. I thank god for her mentorship every day. Like Mary J. Blige says "I'm gonna be the best me, Sorry if it kills you!"[88]

Maria Colompos

In the past three years Dr. Neal's mentorship has allowed me to grow as a scholar in three realms: academics, life, and career. Unquestionably, Dr. Neal has been one of the most influential mentors and has helped me blossom in all three realms. She is a mentor who has gone above and beyond to guarantee a prosperous future and fulfilling career for me. She utilizes multiple strategies to help me shape my scholar identity by allowing me to cling to my cultural ties and past experiences that have impacted my life. Certainly, her guidance and high expectations of me have driven me to excel in every aspect of my life.

In the realm of academics, Dr. Neal has delineated an academic plan for me in order to juggle several academic programs in a four-year period. She has taught me how to maintain a diligent work ethic and time management. In the spring semester of 2015, I remember informing Dr. Neal that I was planning on taking 23 credit hours and she told me that I am fully prepared to accept that challenge. She helped me with my time management skills and always motivated me to undertake such a workload. At the end of the semester, I achieved all A's. She instilled a strong work ethic and never doubted my capabilities. If there was ever a case where I felt that I was overwhelmed with the amount of credit hours, she would encourage me to keep striving. Her encouragement was through her powerful messages and the songs that she would have me listen to in order to connect on a spiritual level. While taking 23 credits in the spring semester of 2015, I focused on the lyrics from a song performed by Kelly Price—"Its My Time." I believed that it was my time to rise and my time to shine.

With her support, I have been able to juggle all of the different academic programs, while presenting at several conferences including the 99th Annual Convention of the Association for the Study of African American Life and History, United Sates Air Force Academy 22nd Annual National Character and Leadership Symposium, Undergraduate Research and Artistry Day at Northern Illinois University, and the Association of Black Women in Higher Education Conference. Being able to present findings at four distinguished conferences, I have perfected my communication, speaking, and networking skills. Additionally, Dr. Neal always informs the Dean of Liberal Arts and Sciences of the progress and contributions that I have made. She shares with others my progress and has ingrained in educators' minds that I am a scholar who is blossoming.

While examining my personal economics, Dr. Neal has assisted me in creating a wealth management plan, which includes retirement planning. When she first told me about wealth building, I thought it was an impossible task. Nonetheless, I trusted her expertise and I know that I will reach my goal. Currently, my plans include investing in real estate.

Without a doubt, Dr. Neal has ensured me that absolutely nothing will stop me from accomplishing my goals, especially in becoming a JAG officer. She has built a strong foundation of hope and belief within me. When I told Dr. Neal about my interest in law school, she introduced me to academic advisors who were a part of the admissions process at Northern Illinois University Law School. I created a strong connection with academic advisors who have helped me immensely in the application process to law school, which would not have been possible without Dr. Neal. She has inspired me to simultaneously pursue a Ph.D. and law degree. Dr. Neal has provided many opportunities for me and I am forever grateful for her believing in my abilities. Her lessons in the three realms—academics, life, and career—have proven to be salient in my perseverance and determination.[89]

Shanell Walter

The mentorship provided by Dr. Neal has been an amazing, inspirational, and phenomenal journey that has helped shape my scholar identity. Her guidance and mentorship has had a noteworthy impact on my career, academics, and personal life.

I have never met anyone like Dr. Neal, a woman of passion and wisdom, great character, and such admirable aspirations to serve. Her willingness to serve the community is truly a gift. She has helped me immensely and has given me encouragement mentally, emotionally, and spiritually. Some people may or may not have someone to steer them into the right direction or to help guide them to the right path. However, she changed that for me. Before meeting her it was like being on a ship, sailing without a captain; Dr. Neal is my captain and has helped me sail my ship to the "Shore of Success."

During my academic career, I have been blessed with the opportunity to go to national conferences to present our research study. As an undergraduate, it is very rare that you are given the opportunity to meet and network with great leaders such as the superintendent of the United States Air Force Academy, Major General Michelle Johnson. Four years ago, writing articles and books, and meeting Sonia Sanchez, a famous poet was inconceivable. Additionally, I met

Judge D' Army Bailey, at the ASALH conference, who gave me his business card and offered to write a letter of recommendation for me to attend law school. These are opportunities I experienced because I have Dr. Neal as my mentor.

She has inspired me to further my education and receive a Ph.D. in communications as well as a law degree. Before I met her I was not sure I wanted to complete my undergraduate education let alone graduate degrees. I did not feel confident or capable of furthering my education beyond a bachelor's degree. Dr. Neal constantly tells me that I am a scholar, reiterating that has enhanced my confidence to keep going further in my career and persevere through life. During our spiritual mentoring meetings, Dr. Neal uses an endarkened feminist approach to empower and uplift us to acknowledge our intellectual capabilities. She also keeps us engaged with learning and committed to improving ourselves to become better scholars.

Over the past three years, the mentorship has made me a stronger person. She has helped me establish a balance with my personal life as a single mother as well as my professional life. She has given me advice on how to manage the many borders within my life. She has given me motherly guidance about young men, and one thing I could never forget her saying is "You are a scholar; I suggest you date a scholar, someone who compliments you." Her mentorship has helped me achieve my dreams and reshape aspirations.[90]

Engaged Learning Highlights

The engaged learning highlights demonstrate the scholars' growth over the past three years in the Endarkened Feminist Mentor Program. We included their involvement in the following areas: (1) undergraduate research; (2) scholar identity development; (3) servant leadership; and (4) career success. We summarized the data to reflect the scholars' collective efforts because we believe in the power of collaboration, teamwork, and shared success.

Undergraduate Research

Conducted Research Study N=1	Publications N=3	Presentations N=4
Conducted Mixed-Methods Research Study **Research Title:** Borders, Bras, & Battles: Sociocultural Perspectives of Female Scholars of Color in ROTC	Co-Authored Book = 1 Co-Authored Academic Journal Article = 1 Co-Authored Chapter in an Edited Book = 1	National / International Conferences = 3 Undergraduate Research Conference at Northern Illinois University = 1

Research Study Summary:

In creative solidarity, we, (1) conducted a mixed-methods research study; (2) wrote three publications; and (3) presented at four conferences

Scholar Identity Development

Honor Societies	Total
Number of Honor Societies	N=11
Number of Leadership Roles in Honor Societies	N=3

Scholarships	Total
Number of Scholarships	N=8

Awards	Total
Number of Awards	N=18

Scholar Identity Summary:

Our scholars demonstrated a successful academic progression since the beginning of the Endarkened Feminist Mentor Program—gaining entry into a total of 11 honor societies over the past three years. Within those honor societies three scholars hold leadership roles and a total of eight scholarships have been distributed to our scholars due to their high academic performance. Of those eight scholarships, all of our scholars received the ROTC Federal Scholarship. Our scholars have collectively earned 18 awards. For example, all have earned the Northern Illinois University (NIU) Leadership Award: Applauding Excellence in Student Career Success. Some of the specific awards and honors include: (1) making the Dean's list multiple semesters; (2) becoming senior leaders in national honor societies; (3) becoming President of the NIU Chapter of Mortar Board; (4) becoming Vice-President of the NIU Chapter of Mortar Board. Cadet Karina Avila speaks to this progression in her scholar identity. She writes: "When I first met with Dr. Neal, my grades were not ideal, and now I can proudly say that I have had the best grades I have ever had."[91]

Servant Leadership

Volunteer Organizations	Total
Number of Organizations	N=13
Number of Leadership Roles in Volunteer Organizations	N=2

Northern Illinois University (NIU) Clubs	Total
Number of NIU Clubs	N=9
Number of Leadership Roles in NIU Clubs	N=3

Other Activities	Total
Number of Other Activities	N=7
Number of Leadership Roles in Other Activities	N=1

Servant Leadership Summary

Since beginning our Endarkened Feminist Mentor Program, our scholars have increased their involvement in the NIU community, local community, and the international community. All of our scholars are contributing in servant leadership activities on and off campus. Some of their leadership activities include: (1) serving as language translators during global humanitarian missions; (2) participating in nine NIU clubs; (3) serving as leaders in two organizations; (4) volunteering in 13 different organizations.

Career Success Conclusion

All three cadets have burgeoned as scholars and leaders since beginning our Endarkened Feminist Mentor Program. All are senior leaders in the U.S. Army ROTC Huskie Battalion at NIU, including the first cadet female battalion commander at NIU. All have received appointments to active duty upon graduation. All have ambitions to continue their education and pursue a Ph.D. and/or a law degree. The following chapter provides an outline of how to engage undergraduates in the research process.

CHAPTER 5
Conducting a Research Study with Undergraduate Scholars

A Practical Guide

This chapter contains specific examples of teacher resources, writing prompts, publicity strategies, excerpts from digital portfolios, research proposals, and select materials we used to engage our undergraduates in research theory. This chapter includes hands-on resources and materials mentors can use to design their own mentoring process or enhance an existing one.

This is not a comprehensive curriculum manual for teaching research methods to undergraduates. It is, however, a supplemental guide that outlines eight practical steps for mentoring undergraduates from the beginning of a research study until the end. We have also included pertinent steps for developing scholar identity in undergraduates such as presenting research at conferences, developing digital portfolios, and creating publicity about the study itself.

The Undergraduate Research Mentoring Process

Step 1	Design a mixed-methods research study organizer (e.g. digital portfolio or binder).
Step 2	Conduct mentoring meetings and research meetings.

Step 3	Create planning charts to assist undergraduates in project management.
Step 4	Conduct the study with undergraduates and write results.
Step 5	Create a publicity plan to publicize the results of the study.
Step 6	Create multi-media power point presentations and present at conferences with undergraduates.
Step 7	Assist undergraduates in publishing the research study.
Step 8	Assist undergraduates in designing a digital portfolio

Step 1: Design and distribute a mixed-methods study organizer (i.e., digital or print), which includes an overview of quantitative research, qualitative research, sample research proposals, published studies, and resource materials. The following web resources provide a basic foundation for undergraduates who are new to the research process. We used the sources listed below to create a mixed-methods study binder (i.e., digital or print) for our undergraduates, which we organized with tabs to separate the materials into specific categories to make the learning process less overwhelming.

Research Resources for Undergraduates

How to write an abstract

The Writing Center, University of North Carolina at Chapel Hill
http://writingcenter.unc.edu/handouts/abstracts/

How to write a literature review

The Writing Center, University of North Carolina at Chapel Hill
https://writingcenter.unc.edu/files/2012/09/Literature-Reviews-The-Writing-Center.pdf

Strengths and Weaknesses of Qualitative and Quantitative Research

Madrigal, D. & McClain, B. (2012). Strengths and Weaknesses of Quantitative and Qualitative Research (Silicon Valley, CA: UXmatters).

http://www.uxmatters.com/mt/archives/2012/09/strengths-and-weaknesses-of-quantitative-and-qualitative-research.php

• **Qualitative Methods**-We used a handbook developed through support provided by the U.S. Agency for International Development (USAD).

Mack, N., Woodsong, C., MacQueen, K.M., Guest, G., & Namely, E. (2005). Qualitative Methods: A Data Collector's Field Guide (Research Triangle Park, NC: Family Health International).

Link to entire handbook can be accessed here:

https://www.urbanreproductivehealth.org/sites/mle/files/datacollectorguideenrh.pdf

• **Quantitative Research**-We used chapters from this textbook published by SAGE, which breaks down the quantitative research process into accessible language for undergraduate readers.

Balnaves, M. & Caputi, P. (2001). Introduction to Quantitative Research Methods (SAGE publications, LTD).

Step 2: Conduct mentoring/research meetings. We held biweekly mentoring meetings that included group discussions and mini-lessons about the research process, and the development of professional and scholar identity. During our meetings, we taught the ABC's of research methodology, and used the Endarkened Feminist Mentor Program (as described in chapter 4) to facilitate goal-setting pertaining to professional and scholar growth. Cadet Shanell Walter spoke to the effect these meetings had on her scholar identity and personal growth, "during our spiritual mentoring meetings, Dr. Neal uses an endarkened feminist approach to empower and uplift us to acknowledge our intellectual capabilities. She also keeps us engaged with learning and committed to improving ourselves to become better scholars."[92]

We covered a variety of material in our mini-lessons on the research process including: (1) how to write research questions; (2) how to write a literature review; (3) how to obtain a good sample; (4) different sampling techniques; (5) choosing a theoretical framework(s); (6) mixed research methods; (7) research methodology; (8) writing an IRB proposal; (9) collecting data; (10) coding data; (11) writing findings; (12) writing results and implications. For more specific examples, see appendices A-D for sample materials.

Step 3: Create planning charts to assist undergraduates in conceptualizing their learning experiences and the steps they need to take to fulfill their professional, scholarly, and economic goals.

Include deadlines and timelines when needed. We created three charts to guide our undergraduate scholars through the scholar identity development process, the graduate school application process, and understanding the importance of personal economics. Cadet Maria Colompos talked about her initial experiences with the economics piece during the planning process:

"While examining my personal economics, Dr. Neal has assisted me in creating a wealth management plan, which includes retirement planning. When she first told me about wealth building, I thought it was an impossible task. Nonetheless, I trusted her expertise and I know that I will reach my goal. Currently, my plans include investing in real estate."[93]

The scholar identity chart also helped the scholars by bracketing the steps they need to take to finish the research study as well as the steps they need to take to successfully apply for graduate school.

Sample Planning Charts:

Professional Identity

Active Duty Selection	Army Branch Assignment	Educational Delay Request
October/November, 2015: Cadets notified	October/November, 2015: Cadets notified	Secure criteria, application due date & apply

Scholar Identity

Undergraduate Research	Graduate Admissions
Select Academic Major	Academic Counseling
Take Research Courses	Criteria for Admissions
Conference Presentations	Resume
Publications	Letters of Recommendation
Digital Portfolios	Personal Statement
	Admission Essay (if applicable)
	Test Preparation & Test
	Apply

Personal Economics

Financial Planning	Career starter loan from Army
Banking Options (e.g. USAA)	529 Plan (to fund dependents' education)

Step 4: Conduct the study with undergraduates and co-write the preliminary results. On the importance of scaffolding: we kept in touch with our undergraduates via email and text messages on a regular basis. That way if the undergraduates had a question or a concern about a specific step in the process, we could address it immediately. We also provided editorial support during the preparation of the study. It is important to edit, provide feedback, and assist in the writing process when conducting research with undergraduates

especially as they develop their scholar identity. Undergraduates can learn, through explicit modeling, how to become academic writers who can compete with other scholars. Ultimately, mentors made the final edits to any document before submitting it to a conference or an academic journal. This is the most salient step because it ensures the success of undergraduates—especially undergraduate scholars who are publishing or presenting for the first time. As they experience their first round of academic success at conferences or through publications, their self-confidence, self-efficacy, and internal locus of control grows stronger—which are some of the core tenets of scholar identity. As Cadet Karina Avila explained:

"The second time we presented was at the U.S. Air Force Academy, and I can honestly say that I had more fun presenting there because I told myself 'Hey, this isn't your first rodeo' and I was less nervous. Plus, seeing the way Dr. Neal presents and captivates the audience is amazing, and I know someday I will have those skills."[94]

Step 5: Develop publicity plan for the study. We cannot over emphasize the importance of promoting the success of undergraduate scholars through appropriate media channels. The Director of College Relations in the College of Education at NIU, Paul Baker, coordinated efforts to develop press releases and communication with reporters. We prepared press releases to highlight two of our conference presentations at the 99th Annual Conference for the Association for the Study of African American Life and History (ASALH) as well as the 22nd Annual National Character and Leadership Symposium (NCLS). Northern Illinois University (NIU) published an article about the undergraduates in its online news source titled NIU Today. In addition, publicity can go much farther in the way mentors share their scholars' progress with other colleagues. As Cadet Maria Colompos said enthusiastically:

Dr. Neal always informs the Dean of Liberal Arts and Sciences of the progress and contributions that I have made. She shares with others my progress and has ingrained in educators' minds that I am a scholar who is blossoming.[95]

Step 6: Create multi-media presentations and present at academic conferences with undergraduate scholars. Print out all of the electronic presentations and distribute to the undergraduates in advance, so they can practice presenting their research. The quality of the power point slides, images, and media clips are a prerequisite for delivering a dynamic presentation at an academic conference with undergraduates.

We designed presentations with high-resolution pictures / JPGs; high definition music videos (MP4s); and high quality audio of interviews (MP3s). We also used social media—(Twitter) to engage conference participants and Twitter followers. We tweeted live from the sessions and collected all comments using the tool—Storify. We used this qualitative feedback from conference participants and twitter followers as vital assessment data to enhance future presentations.

Step 7: Assist undergraduates in publishing the research study and any other academic articles pertaining to their scholarly interests. Provide writing prompts that are grounded in the experiential or musical—prompts which will guide and sustain them through the publishing process. We provided specific writing instructions to guide our undergraduates through two major projects: the completion of a book chapter and the completion of a journal article for a peer-reviewed academic publication. All three scholars reported that the writing prompts were crucial in helping them finish the projects. Cadet Shanell Walter shared the joy and benefits of meeting famous poets and civil rights activists/authors along the way:

"Four years ago, writing articles and books, and meeting Sonia Sanchez, a famous poet was inconceivable. Additionally, I met Judge D' Army Bailey, at the ASALH conference, who gave me his business card and offered to write a letter of recommendation for me to attend law school. These are opportunities I experienced because I have Dr. Neal as my mentor."[96]

Step 8: Provide tools to assist scholars in developing individual digital portfolios that will document their success throughout the rest of their career. The scholars may use various digital/computer tools such as a flash drive, a desktop folder, or a Google document, to digitally archive and organize their accomplishments. (Remind scholars to back up all files). These archives may evolve to include some of the following: (1) programs from academic conferences where they presented their research; (2) copies of their publications; (3) photos from conferences of them interacting with distinguished scholars; (4) and snapshots of books autographed by the authors; (5) copies of newspaper articles about their successful endeavors; (6) copies of press releases about their publications, etc. Make sure all digital articles and press releases (ones that are only available online) are printed out and then copied before uploading them to a digital file as links rarely stay active over time.

AFTERWORD

Lifting as We Climb:
A Mentorship Model

By Karsonya Wise Whitehead

Learning how to stand up in a crooked room is not easy. It is challenging. It is hard and it can be lonely, very lonely, if you are trying to do it alone. It is also necessary, as Audre Lorde once wrote, because this struggle teaches us how to "bear the intimacy of scrutiny, and to flourish within it." This struggle to stand up, to want to be free, to want to carve your own path exists inside the hearts and minds of every sister scholar. It is probably what drove us into the academy. We were born with questions that we had to answer, paths that we had to pursue, and dreams that we had to realize. We were told that we were special and were encouraged along the way to believe that the path to success was straight and narrowly defined. Slowly, as we continued to move along the path, we realized that something was off; not quite right, and yet, we could not name it. We found that the room that we thought was straight, was actually crooked and the path that we thought was clear, was not. Thus, we began the work to find an unrestricted path, where we could grow and exhale. A place where we would no longer question our abilities or accept the limitations that others placed upon our lives.

When we finally found that path, we realized that it was only through the work of our mentors and through the application of an endarkened feminist epistemology, that we began to find ourselves. We began to remember the joy that came from learning and the sense of belonging that we used to have. We began to realize that we were standing on the shoulders of sister scholars who had come before us. Their lives and their experiences standing tall as guideposts to help us to bring our tiny ships of knowledge to port.

Mentoring is a process and a labor of love. And those who do it well, understand that the work to pour love, light, truth, and hope into young scholars is a sacrifice. It takes time to build relationships; it takes work to nurture a young scholar; and, it takes a lot of concentrated effort to help to prepare the next generation of leaders. La Vonne Neal, Alicia Moore, and Sarah Militz-Frielink have done the hard work for us. They have mentored three young women, documented the process (both the successes and the failures), and made it available for us. The endarkened feminist epistemology is a road map and for any senior scholar who is interested in helping to prepare the next generation, it is a bible (of sorts) that can be pulled out and used as a reference, time and time again. It is that tool that we have been waiting for, the one that will help us to tear down these crooked rooms, once and for all, and build spaces where every scholar is able to stand.

APPENDIX A

Excerpts of the initial written results of our study (Phase 1)

Abstract

This mixed-methods study examined sociocultural perspectives of three undergraduate female scholars who are simultaneously training in an ROTC program. Using an endarkened feminist framework, this study examined a new mentorship program and the factors, which influenced the scholars' decision to pursue academic research endeavors and military leadership positions. Additionally, this study ascertained the racial, ethnic, gender, and language challenges, which have contributed to the ROTC cadets' development as leaders and scholars.

Study Themes

Upon the completion of the data sorting and coding, the following themes emerged from the scholars' self-interviews about their experiences in ROTC: mentors matter, empowerment to achieve goals, scholar identity development, gender, race & language challenges, persistence and resilience.

Preliminary Findings

All of the scholars reported that being in an endarkened feminist mentorship program helps them navigate gender, race, ethnicity, or language challenges more confidently and successfully. The scholars reported that when leaders set high expectations and believe in their capabilities, the cadets are more likely to stay in the military, set high goals, and be successful. Despite any challenges the scholars have had with respect to policies and procedures, they indicated that ROTC training has helped them persevere and succeed academically.

One scholar indicated that the military hair policy AR 670-1, which bans certain naturally texturized hairstyles, causes an undo financial burden as the authorized hairstyles are expensive to maintain.

The scholars indicated that staying focused on their career goals, and having a positive attitude helped them deal with race, ethnicity, gender, or language barriers. One scholar reported that she believed her diverse background improved the way she interacted with international students on campus. Another scholar said that having a diverse background helps her to teach others about the importance of appreciating different cultural norms and values.

Implications

-Mentorship programs should continue to be a part of undergraduate curriculum in both military and academic settings.

-Hair policy AR 670-1 should be re-visited to be more inclusive of naturally texturized hairstyles.

-Leaders in the military and academia could benefit from more diversity and cultural agility trainings.

References

Butler, Judith. 1999. *Gender trouble: Feminism and the subversion of identity*. New York: Routledge.

hooks, bell. 1984. *Feminist theory: From margin to center*. Boston, MA: South End Press.

Lorde, Audre. 1984. *Sister outsider: essays and speeches*. Trumansburg, NY: Crossing Press.

Lewis, Reina, and Sara Mills. 2003. *Feminist postcolonial theory: a reader.* New York: Routledge.

Mohanty, Chandra Talpade. 2003. *Feminism without borders: decolonizing theory, practicing solidarity.* Durham: Duke University Press.

Richie, Beth. 2012. *Arrested justice: Black women, violence, and America's prison nation.* New York: New York University Press.

Said, Edward W. 1993. *Culture and imperialism.* New York: Knopf.

U.S. Department of Defense http://www.defense.gov/.

APPENDIX B
Sample News Article

The Power of Three plus Three: Researchers from NIU, University of Illinois at Chicago, Southwestern University collaborate[1]

Scholars from NIU, the University of Illinois at Chicago and Southwestern University collaborate on ground-breaking research study.

The power of three plus three in a research study has come to fruition as scholars from three different universities in the United States and three different colleges at NIU co-authored a study titled "Borders, Bras, and Battles: Sociocultural Perspectives of Female Scholars of Color in ROTC."

The design of the study began when La Vonne I. Neal, dean of the NIU College of Education, proposed the idea to her research assistant, Sarah Militz-Frielink, a doctoral candidate in the curriculum studies program at UIC.

Neal and Militz-Frielink began penning the research proposal along with three ROTC undergraduate scholars at NIU. The ROTC cadets/scholars are Maria Colompos and Shanell Walter, undergraduates in the College; and Karina Avila, an undergraduate in

---

1 NIU Today, *The Power of 3+3: Researchers from NIU, University of Illinois at Chicago, Southwestern University collaborate*, December 17, 2014, http://www.niutoday. info/2014/12/17/the-power-of-3-3/. (Reprinted with permission).

the College of Health and Human Sciences.

Since Day One of the proposal writing process, Avila, Colompos and Walter have taken the research opportunity very seriously.

Colompos elaborated on their experience working with Dean Neal, who is the lead researcher on the study. "Dean Neal is a data-driven, mission focused leader who has sparked the genius within us," she said.

Lt. Col. David Dosier, a professor of military science at NIU, spoke to the beneficial impact that ROTC and scholarly activities at NIU have had Avila, Colompos and Walter.

"Over the past three years, I've had the pleasure of watching the combination of their scholarly pursuits and ROTC leadership training have a clear, positive impact on their professional and personal growth," he said.

Their collaborative efforts did not end there.

Alicia L. Moore, a member of the U.S. Army Command and General Staff College Advisory Board and holds the Cargill Endowed Professorship at Southwestern University, also contributed to the overall design of the study.

"The study ultimately benefits from the expertise of researchers across three different universities and three different colleges at Northern Illinois University," Militz-Frielink said. "It is truly an interdisciplinary effort."

The authors of the study recently presented their initial findings at the 99th annual Association for the Study of African American Life History convention in Memphis.

"There is a paucity of research on female scholars of color in the military and the challenges they navigate," Moore said. "This study is paving the way for a whole new body of literature on women in the military."

Phase One of the study examined sociocultural perspectives of undergraduate female scholars of color who are simultaneously training in an ROTC program. The study draws upon Black feminist theory, critical race theory and post-colonial studies.

"The first phase of our study involved participatory action research – where three female cadets of color conducted self-interviews and coded the results," Militz-Frielink said. "We discovered that the military instilled in the cadets a sense of empowerment to achieve high academic goals and skills to effectively manage challenges."

The second phase of the study will include an analysis of the historical presence of women of color in the military and interviews with female military leaders of color who hold positions in academia.

The authors of the study hope their research will contribute to the larger discussion on social justice and civil rights in America.

"Within the continuous struggle for civil rights, the sociocultural perspectives, stories, and scholarly endeavors of military women of color should be published as salient parts of the historical movement for equality in America," Neal said.

Currently, the authors have a contract with a publisher; they plan to publish a book that highlights their findings and gives examples of how to engage undergraduates in the research process.

"I support cross-university and cross-campus collaborations," said Alfred Tatum, dean of the UIC College of Education. "They are important for our doctoral candidates – particularly those who engage undergraduate students in applying research theory."

APPENDIX C
Sample Press Release

Sample Press Release:

Recruitment, retention, perseverance, and the development of scholar identity in female ROTC cadets of color are just a few of the factors analyzed in a new research study about women in the military.

Scholars from Northern Illinois University (NIU) Southwestern University, and University of Illinois at Chicago (UIC) have been collaborating on this ground-breaking study that focuses on sociocultural perspectives of female scholars of color in ROTC."

At the end of February, five of the six researchers will travel to Colorado Springs to present their findings at the 22nd Annual National Character and Leadership Symposium (NCLS). NCLS is one of the premier national symposiums in the area of character development that brings together distinguished scholars, armed forces leaders, corporate presidents and others to explore various dimensions of character and leadership.

The researchers presenting at NCLS include La Vonne I. Neal, dean of the College of Education at NIU, Sarah Militz-Frielink, a doctoral candidate in the curriculum studies program at UIC and three ROTC undergraduate scholars at NIU. The ROTC cadets/scholars are Maria Colompos and Shanell Walter, undergraduates in the College of Liberal Arts and Sciences; and Karina Avila, an undergraduate in the College of Health and Human Sciences.

The commitment of Avila, Colompos and Walter has garnered the attention of a book publisher. As a result, the researchers are writing a book that highlights their findings and gives examples of how to engage undergraduates in the research process.

Their research is extremely valuable because it demonstrates the impact of mentorship on ROTC cadets of color and factors which impact retention and recruitment of women in the military. The book will also illuminate the impact of mentorship on the development of scholar identity and the cadets' ability to persevere through dual missions—in the military and academia.

Avila spoke to the impact of mentorship on the development of scholar identity, and retention in ROTC. "Dean Neal is one the greatest role models I have ever had. Without her believing in me, and giving me these opportunities, I would not be where I am today."

The research data was collected in two phases, and the scholars presented results from the first phase at the Association for the study of African American Life and History (ASALH) conference in September 2014.

"The first phase of our study involved participatory action research – where three female cadets of color conducted self-interviews and coded the results," Militz-Frielink said.

"The second phase of the study included an analysis of the historical presence of women of color in the military and interviews with female military leaders of color who hold positions in academia."

The authors of the study believe their research will contribute to the larger discussion on social justice and civil rights in America.

"Within the continuous struggle for civil rights, the sociocultural perspectives, stories, and scholarly endeavors of military women of color should be published as salient parts of the historical movement for equality in America," Neal said.

APPENDIX D
Writing Prompts

Sample Writing Prompts for a Book Chapter in an Edited Book

Your assignment is as follows: write at least 10 pages about your experiences being mentored by Dr. Neal. Draw inspiration from Cynthia B. Dillard's book titled, *Learning to (Re) member the Things We've Learned to Forget.* Peruse the attached book prospectus. Use the transnational endarkened feminist framework, which is outlined in the book prospectus, to guide the writing process.

We have also assigned songs for inspiration. Click on the link that is next to your name, and watch the music video for your assigned song; study the song lyrics. You may quote the song lyrics in your book chapter, quote sections of Cynthia B. Dillard's book, and quote poetry that helps you write about Dr. Neal's impact on your life. You should draw upon poetry and literature to write about your experiences.

We have compiled a series of photos from the ASALH conference to inspire your writing process as well. Look at the photos of you with poet Sonia Sanchez, ASALH President Daryl Michael Scott, and think about meeting them as one of the layers of your experience. Not only did you interact with them in person, but you also had the experience of connecting deeply with their writings. Remember when we met D'army Bailey, the founder of the National Civil Rights Museum the same day we visited the museum on the Memphis tour? That is another layer of our experience that Dr. Neal facilitated. Visiting a historical museum about civil rights and interacting with the founder of that museum during a book signing on the same day. Reflect on what you did at the conference, what you learned while you were there, and how Dr. Neal modeled for us and taught us how to network at a conference. Draw upon your experiences at the restaurants, Dr. Neal's other mentees you met (our success entourage), and the meaningful conversations you had with them while we enjoyed the local culinary fare.

Here are the tentative themes of the chapters and descriptions you will be writing for the book:

Karina Avila's chapter illustrates the life-changing impact that a former military intelligence officer had on a disillusioned ROTC scholar. Chapter three outlines how mentors can channel their life experiences to inspire undergraduates to succeed both academically and professionally.

Maria Colompos' chapter is a story of how a dedicated ROTC scholar overcomes fears from her past experiences in school and summons the courage to apply for law school while finishing an innovative research project. This chapter shows how mentors can empower women to use endarkened feminism to cultivate their own authentic academic identities.

Shanell Walter's chapter shows how mentors can empower women to construct paradigms that encompass and embody [their] cultural and spiritual understandings, memories, and the histories that shape [their] epistemologies and ways of being" (Dillard, 2012, p. 58).

Sample Writing Prompt for Academic Article:

You will co-author a paper to be submitted to the *Black History Bulletin*.

Your assignment is as follows:

Collaboratively write at least 10 pages about your roles as current ROTC leaders and future military leaders—specifically your role to PROTECT ALL GROUNDS. You can chronicle pieces of military history that involved battles fought on hallowed grounds—especially hallowed grounds involved in the Civil Rights Movement and the subsequent battles that ensued.

For example, during the historical struggle for civil rights the military has been called upon to protect protestors who were marching for freedom and Black students entering desegregated schools for the first time. These Civil Rights battles have taken place at various grounds/sites in America from Little Rock, Arkansas to Selma to Montgomery, Alabama.

For inspiration, draw upon the lyrics or just listen to the following songs:

"We shall Overcome"

"Woke up this Morning with my Mind Stayed on Freedom"
"Ain't Gonna Let Nobody Turn me Round"

Many of these songs were sung during the civil rights battles when U.S. soldiers were protecting the marchers, students or protestors.

Feel free to draw upon poetry and literature to write about your military leadership roles or these battles.

Think about the values you are learning through the NIU ROTC Huskie Battalion—**Leadership Through Knowledge, swiftness, defiance, and power,** and how you apply leadership through knowledge. You are all soldiers sojourning through hallowed grounds. You can use a variety of hallowed sites to help you frame this article for the *Black History Bulletin.* You can also describe the Hallowed Grounds you visited this year as military researchers—**The Tuskegee Airmen Exhibit at USAFA,** the **National Civil Rights Museum in Memphis** where Dr. Martin Luther King, Jr. was assassinated. You can also write about the historical role of the military in protecting the **Little Rock**

Nine students in Arkansas, etc. (Little Rock Museum is a Hallowed Ground).

In addition, please include some hallowed grounds in Illinois as part of this historical article. You can organize the piece through Hallowed Grounds in Memphis, Colorado, and Illinois, You can also write about Little Rock, Selma or Montgomery.

Here is a great website you can use to help you think/write about Hallowed Grounds: http://www.hallowedground.org/

Please write in Chicago manual style in a word document, which is a footnote system. Here is a link to the Chicago manual style quick guide that shows you how to write your footnotes for books, articles, journals, websites, etc. http://www.chicagomanualofstyle.org/tools_citationguide.html

Follow the numbered (footnote) examples on how to write your footnotes.

The deadline for this co-written article is May 15, 2015.

Please make sure you read the most recent copy of the *Black History Bulletin* that we gave you in your Colorado Springs presentation folder. This will help you become more acquainted with the style of the *Black History Bulletin*.

ENDNOTES

1 Melissa V. Harris-Perry, *Sister Citizen: Shame, Stereotypes, and Black Women in America* (New Haven: Yale University Press, 2011).

2 Ibid.

3 bell hooks, *Sisters of the Yam: Black Women and Self-Recovery* (Boston: South End Press, 1993), 161-162.

4 Maxine Greene, *Releasing the Imagination: Essays on Education, the Arts, and Social Change* (San Francisco: Jossey-Bass Publishers), 22.

5 F.H. Ramey, "Mentoring: It's Role in the Advancement of Women Administrators in Higher Education,"*Black Issues in Higher Education*, 10 no. 17 (1993): 116.

6 See chapter 2 for more a more detailed review of the military literature on mentoring.

7 W. Brad Johnson and Gene R. Andersen, "Formal Mentoring in the U.S. Military: Research Evidence, Lingering Questions, and Recommendations," *Naval War College Review*, 63 no. 2 (2010): 5.

8 Maryann Jacobi, "Mentoring and Undergraduate Academic Success: A Literature Review," *Review of Educational Research*, 61 no. 4 (1991): 505-532.

9 Gloria Crisp and Irene Cruz, "Mentoring College Students: A Critical Review of the Literature between 1990 and 2007," *Research in High Education,* 50 no. 6 (2009): 525-545.

10 Susan Gershenfeld, "A Review of Undergraduate Mentoring Programs," *Review of Educational Research,* 84 no. 3 (2014): 365-391.

11 We delve into the theoretical framework-- endarkened feminist epistemology--in Chapter 4 and provide a practical guide for researching with and mentoring undergraduates in Chapter 5 using this framework.

12 Vera John-Steiner and Holbrook Mahn, "Sociocultural Perspectives to Learning and Development: A Vygotskian Framework," *Educational Psychologist,* 31 no. ¾ (1996): 191.

13 Chesler, Mark A., Kristie A. Ford, Joseph A. Galura, and Jessica M. Charbeneau, "Peer Facilitators as Border Crossers in Community Service Learning," *Teaching Sociology*, 34 no. 4 (2006): 341-356.

14 Whiting as cited in Gilman Whiting, "The Scholar Identity Institute: Guiding Darnel and Other Black Males," *Gifted Child Today,* 32 no. 4 (2009): 55.

15 Gilman Whiting, "Gifted Black Males: Understanding and Decreasing Barriers to Achievement and Identity," *Roeper Review*, 31 no. 4 (October 2009): 224-233.

16 Conceptual model: Characteristics of a scholar identity. Note: Adapted from "Promoting a Scholar Identity among African-American Males: Implications for Gifted Education," by Gilman W. Whiting, *Gifted Education Press Quarterly*, 20 no. 3 (2006):2–6.

17 Karina Avila, Self-Interview, May 15, 2015.

18 Maria Colompos, Self-Interview, May 15, 2015.

19 Shanell Walter, Self-Interview, May 15, 2015.

20 Lee A. Bell, "Theoretical Foundations for Social Justice Education," in *Teaching for Diversity and Social Justice,* ed. Maurianne Adams, Lee A. Bell, and Pat Griffin (New York, NY:Routledge, 2007), 65-66.

21 Audre Lorde, *Sister Outsider: Essays and Speeches* (Trumansburg: Crossing Press, 1984).

22 Adams, Bell and Griffin, *Teaching for Diversity and Social Justice*, 47.

23 Adams, Bell and Griffin, *Teaching for Diversity and Social Justice*, 46.

24 See the scholarship of Joseph E. Flynn for a better understanding of systems of oppression, socialization, the media, and social justice.

25 Rubin A. Gaztambide-Fernandez, "Toward Creative Solidarity in the "Next" Moment of Curriculum Work" in *Curriculum Studies Handbook The Next Moment* ed. Erik Malewski (New York: Routledge, 2010), 85.

26 Maryann Jacobi, "Mentoring and Undergraduate Academic Success," 505-532.

27 Gloria Crisp and Irene Cruz, "Mentoring College Students," 525-545.

28 Susan Gershenfeld, "A Review of Undergraduate Mentoring Programs," 365-391.

29 Jacobi, "Mentoring and Undergraduate Academic Success," 505-532.

30 Ibid.

31 Ibid, 518.

32 Ibid., 519.

33 Ibid.

34 F. H. Ramey, Mentoring: Its role in the advancement of women administrators in higher education. *Black Issues in Higher Education,* 10 no. 17 (1993): 116.

35 Regina Lewis, Interview with Authors, September 27, 2014.

36 Gloria Crisp and Irene Cruz, "Mentoring College Students," 525-545.

37 Ruth Enid Zambrana, Rashawn Ray, Michelle M. Espino, Corinne Castro, Beth Douthirt Cohen, Jennifer Eliason, "Don't Leave Us Behind: The Importance of Mentoring for Underrepresented Minority Faculty," *American Educational Research Journal,* 52 no. 1 (2015): 40-72.

38 Alicia L. Moore, "African American Early Childhood Teachers' Decisions to Refer African American Students," *International Journal of Qualitative Studies,* 15 no. 6 (2002): 631-652.

39 Karina Avila.

40 Maria Colompos.

41 Shanell Walter.

42 Foster as cited in Moore, "African American Early Childhood Teachers' Decisions," 648.

43 Gloria Crisp and Irene Cruz, "Mentoring College Students,"525-545.

44 For an introduction to post-colonial theory see Edward W. Said, *Culture and Imperialism* (New York: Knopf, 1993). For an introduction to critical race theory see *Critical Race Theory: The Key Writings that Formed the Movement* eds. Kimberle Crenshaw, et al (New York: The New Press, 1995).

45 Susan Gershenfeld, "A Review of Undergraduate Mentoring Programs," 384.

46 Ibid.

47 Susan Gershenfeld, "A Review of Undergraduate Mentoring Programs," 365-391.

48 Regina Lewis.

49 Stephen B. Knouse, and Schuyler C. Webb, "Unique Types of Mentoring for Diverse Groups in the Military," *Review Of Business,* 21 no. 1/2 (Summer 2000): 48. Business Source Elite, EBSCOhost (accessed June 26, 2015).

50 Athena, "Greek Mythology," http://www.greekmythology.com/Olympians/Athena/athena.html.

51 Ibid.

52 W. Brad Johnson and Gene R. Andersen, "Formal Mentoring in the U.S. Military: Research Evidence, Lingering Questions, and Recommendations," *Naval War College Review,* 63 no. 2 (2010): 5.

53 AFI 36-3401, Air Force Mentoring, 1 June 2000, 1.

54 U.S. Department of the Air Force as cited in Frank C. Budd, "Mentoring in the U.S. Air Force: A Cornerstone for Success through Organizational Transformation," *Performance Improvement,* 46 no. 3 (2008) 16.

55 Todd R. Lancaster, *Air Force Mentoring: Developing Leaders.* Paper submitted to the Air Command and Staff College Maxwell Air Force Base, Air University, April 2003.

56 Budd, Mentoring in the U.S. Air Force, 18.

57 Ibid., 19.

58 Colonel Gail Colvin, Interview with Authors, September 15, 2015

59 Gregg F. Martin, George E. Reed, Ruth B. Collins, and Cortez K. Dial, "The Road to Mentoring: Paved with Good Intentions," *Parameters,* (Autumn 2002): 117.

60 Ibid., 4.

61 US Army report as cited in Gregg F. Martin, George E. Reed, Ruth B. Collins, and Cortez K. Dial, "The Road to Mentoring: Paved with Good Intentions," *Parameters,* (Autumn 2002): 117.

62 Stephanie C. Payne and Ann H. Huffman, "A Longitudinal Examination of the Influence of Mentoring on Organizational Commitment and Turnover," *Academy of Management Journal,* 48 no. 1 (2005): 165.

63 Knouse, et. al, "Unique Types of Mentoring for Diverse Groups in the Military," 49.

64 Ibid., 49.

65 Emerald M. Archer, "The Power of Gendered Stereotypes in the U.S. Marine Corps," *Armed Forces & Society,* 39 no. 2 (2012): 375.

66 Ibid.

67 Regina Lewis. September 27, 2014.

68 Archer, "The Power of Gendered Stereotypes,"50.

69 Bret T. Baker, Susan P. Hocevar, and W. Brad Johnson, "The Prevalence and Nature of Service Academy Mentoring: A Study of Navy Midshipmen," *Military Psychology* (Taylor & Francis Ltd), 15 no. 4 (October 2003): 273-283. Academic Search Complete, EBSCOhost (accessed June 1, 2015).

70 Ibid., 279.

71 Colonel Gail Colvin.

72 Colonel Gail Colvin.

73 Ibid.

74 Colonel Gail Colvin.

75 Cynthia B. Dillard, "Cultural Considerations in Paradigm Proliferation." Paper presented at the Annual Meeting of the American Educational Research Association, New Orleans, LA. (2000), 2.

76 Cynthia B. Dillard, *On Spiritual Strivings: Transforming an African American Woman's Academic Life* (New York: State University of New York Press, 2006), 3.

77 Ibid.

78 Ledisi, (song lyrics) *Pieces of Me,* http://www.azlyrics.com/lyrics/ledisi/piecesofme.html.

79 Shanell Walter.

80 Ibid.

81 Karina Avila.

82 Dillard, *On Spiritual Strivings,* 3.

83 James Joseph Scheurich and Michelle D. Young, "Coloring Epistemologies: Are Our Research Epistemologies Racially Biased?" *Educational Researcher,*

26 no. 4 (1997): 4-16.

84 Ibid., 5.

85 Army Regulation 600-20, "Army Command Policy," http://www.apd.army.mil/pdffiles/r600_20.pdf/.

86 Army Regulation 670-1, "Wear and Appearance of Army Insignia and Uniforms," http://www.apd.army.mil/pdffiles/r670_1.pdf.

87 Mary J. Blige, (song lyrics) *Doubt,* http://www.metrolyrics.com/doubt-lyrics-mary-j-blige.html.

88 Karina Avila, Self-Interview, August 28, 2015.

89 Maria Colompos, Self-Interview, August 28, 2015.

90 Shanell Walter, Self-Interview, August 28, 2015.

91 Karina Avila.

92 Shanell Walter.

93 Maria Colompos.

94 Karina Avila.

95 Maria Colompos.

96 Shanell Walter.

Apprentice House is the country's only campus-based, student-staffed book publishing company. Directed by professors and industry professionals, it is a nonprofit activity of the Communication Department at Loyola University Maryland.

Using state-of-the-art technology and an experiential learning model of education, Apprentice House publishes books in untraditional ways. This dual responsibility as publishers and educators creates an unprecedented collaborative environment among faculty and students, while teaching tomorrow's editors, designers, and marketers.

Outside of class, progress on book projects is carried forth by the AH Book Publishing Club, a co-curricular campus organization supported by Loyola University Maryland's Office of Student Activities.

Eclectic and provocative, Apprentice House titles intend to entertain as well as spark dialogue on a variety of topics. Financial contributions to sustain the press's work are welcomed. Contributions are tax deductible to the fullest extent allowed by the IRS.

To learn more about Apprentice House books or to obtain submission guidelines, please visit www.apprenticehouse.com.

Apprentice House
Communication Department
Loyola University Maryland
4501 N. Charles Street
Baltimore, MD 21210
Ph: 410-617-5265 • Fax: 410-617-2198
info@apprenticehouse.com • www.apprenticehouse.com